Sibelius

Cover design and art direction by Pearce Marchbank Studio.
Cover photography by Julian Hawkins.

Printed and bound in Hungary

© David Burnett-James 1989.
This edition published in 1989 by Omnibus Press, a division of Book Sales Limited.

Hardback
Order No. OP44163
ISBN 0.7119.1061.8

Softback
Order No. OP45004
ISBN 0.7119.1683.7

Exclusive Distributors:
Book Sales Limited,
8/9 Frith Street,
London W1V 5TZ,
England.
Music Sales Pty Limited,
120 Rothschild Avenue,
Rosebery,
Sydney,
NSW 2018,
Australia.
To The Music Trade Only:
Music Sales Limited,
8/9 Frith Street,
London W1V 5TZ,
England.
Music Sales Corporation,
24 East 22nd Street,
New York,
NY10010,
U.S.A.

The Illustrated Lives of the Great Composers.

Sibelius

David Burnett-James

Omnibus Press
London/New York/Sydney/Cologne

Other titles in the series

Contents

Acknowledgements

My most grateful thanks are due to the Collection Abo Akademis of the Sibelius Museum for the provision of photographs and documents without which this book would be even more incomplete than it inevitably is. And my particular thanks go to Iner Jakobsson-Wärn, the casual amanuens whose ready co-operation at all times and in all contexts has been invaluable. Also to the Finnish publishers K. J. Gummerus, Otava Publishing Company and Lehtikuva Oy who provided further pictures for the book.

Although efforts have been made to trace the present copyright holders of photographs, the publishers apologise in advance for any unintentional omission or neglect and will be pleased to insert the appropriate acknowledgement to companies or individuals in any subsequent edition of this book.

SIBELIUS: his life and times

Sibelius (centre) with his
brother and sister.

Chapter 1

Preliminaries

The Voice of the North: it came into music, like so many other regional and national 'voices', in the latter half of the nineteenth century—with, it might be argued, first the Norwegian Ole Bull (1810-1880) and the Dane Niels Gade (1817-90) followed by another Norwegian, Edvard Grieg (1843-1907). But none of these spoke with the full and full-throated voice of the North. The strongest of the northern voices at that period was not in music at all but in drama, in the work and person of Henrik Ibsen, also Norwegian. In music it had to wait for the coming of the Finn Jean (or Jan) Sibelius for the outright power and overwhelming presence of the European North to make its total impact. After all, did not Claude Debussy once wickedly, probably a little maliciously but with a sharp barb of truth, describe the music of Grieg as 'a pink *fondant* stuffed with snow'? But Sibelius—that was a different matter: nothing of comfort stuffed with snow, no

The house where Sibelius was born in Tavastehus/ Hämeenlinna.

A view of the Sibelius
house at Loviisa with the
church in the background.

Loviisa.

Sibelius's paternal great grandfather appears to have been a farmer from central Finland who moved south to Lapinjärvi (or Lappträsk) and took the name
'Sibbe' from the area of land he worked. His son and Sibelius's grandfather
moved to Loviisa, a town on the coast to the east of Helsinki. Loviisa became
the family home of the Sibeliuses and during his youth Sibelius and his brother
and sister frequently went there.

agreeable skating on nicely frozen ponds, no indulgence of Christmas card winter, but the harsh voice and reality of the frozen wastes, the burdened forests, the whiplash of winds that strike to kill; the barren expanses of spirit as well as of landscape. That is not all; naturally there is a good deal more to it, much more to Jean Sibelius than his one-time reputation as a kind of crude, chest-thumping Tarzan of the North or a musical merchant in icepacks and old bones. Tenderness and gentleness are by no means absent from the music of Sibelius; warmth and generosity of spirit are by no means incapable of thawing the predominant freeze of the familiar Sibelius atmosphere. And above and beyond all that, all responses to nature and landscape (and Sibelius himself was unusually aware of the effect of the Finnish landscape and its geological constitution) there is the sense that in the music of Sibelius a rare and specific area of human consciousness becomes manifest. To this we shall come later and examine in its turn as we progress through the succession of Sibelius's compositions.

He was born on 8 December 1865 at Tavastehus (which is the Swedish appellation of the Finnish town of Hämeenlinna in the province of Hame: at that time many parts of Finland were not

The Sibelius house at Loviisa.

only Swedish territory but also Swedish speaking), and died at his villa at Järvenpää outside Helsinki, where he lived all the latter part of his life, on 20 September 1957. These two dates define the extremes of the parameters of Sibelius's life. It will thus be seen that he lived an exceptionally long time. On the other hand, he did not have an unusually long career as a composer: he wrote virtually nothing during the last thirty or so years of his life, although he remained to the end a distinguished and honoured

11

Sibelius's father.

figure in the contemporary musical world. This in itself has led to some distortion of historical perspectives. Although he did not die until well into the 1950s, he ceased composing during the 1920s. He thus belongs to an earlier generation of European composers than his dates may superficially indicate. Something of the same might have been said of Richard Strauss if that composer had not gone on producing new music (new in date though hardly in style) right up to the end of a long life (he died in 1949 aged eighty-five). Gustav Mahler on the other hand died at just under fifty-one in 1911, which again tends to distort the historical perspectives, this time by foreshortening. One might also mention Edward Elgar, also of that same generation who

Sibelius's mother.

died at seventy-seven in 1934 (the year in which Delius and Holst also died) having written virtually nothing of substance since the death of his wife in 1920. So Jean Sibelius stands in the history book in a way which straddles an entire age of musical and sociological and political history though his active career was contained within a shorter period. This in itself produced a particular kind of distortion: because Sibelius lived on for thirty years after his life's work was accomplished, when the inevitable 'reaction' against him set in after his death it came at a time when musical history had moved on farther and faster than is usual in such cases. Add that to the fact that the whole ethic and aesthetic of art and life had changed radically, not only since his creative maturity but in the period of his 'silence', and it is easy to see how the misconceptions arose, and why they arose, and why he came to appear 'old fashioned' and creatively superseded, one of the musical unburied dead. His actual achievement and its precise nature, no less than its outward appearance, invited critical misunderstanding amounting at times to demonstrable incompetence. And it was not helped by some of the exaggerated praise and hyperbolic claims made for him by certain critics, mostly British but some American. All reputations have to be constantly reassessed; that of Sibelius in a number of respects presented an unusual problem.

His family was of the Swedish speaking petite bourgeoisie, his father a military doctor at Hämeenlinna.

He was named Johan Julius Christian but as a boy he was always known in the family as Janne. He was the middle child of three, a sister, Linda, preceding him by two years, a brother called Christian following him by four years and destined also to become a musician in his youth although he later qualified as a doctor and practised psychiatry with some material success. Also important in the young Sibelius's life were two uncles, one Uncle Johan, a sea captain who travelled the world and who used the French form of his Christian name when on his travels and by it inspired the young Sibelius to use Jean also; the other, Uncle Pehr, a keen amateur musician and successful businessman.

Although in some ways Sibelius was socially and materially well favoured in his family, disaster was not long in striking. As early as 1867, less than two years after Janne's birth, his father died in a typhoid epidemic. It seems clear that his constitution had already been weakened by drink and dissipation and he left behind him such a tangle of debt that his widow was almost immediately faced with an action for bankruptcy. However, she was not a woman to be put down by the vicissitudes of life, and she soon pulled matters together, obtained some small concessions from the creditors, returned to her own mother's home, also in Hämeenlinna, and kept her family on an even keel. There were also grandmothers, both maternal and paternal, with whom the boy spent time through a childhood which, despite the deprivation, appears to have been reasonably happy and untroubled.

He revealed early musical tendencies, though there was little to indicate that he would become a world famous musician; he was nothing like a child prodigy in any sense. There was an aunt, Evelina, who encouraged the children in music and all three played—sister Linda and himself the piano, brother Christian the cello. It was not until he began violin lessons with Gustav Levander, the bandmaster at Hämeenlinna, that his true musical

14

Sibelius's Uncle Pehr.

course began to be set. Even then it did not set accurately at once: he nurtured a serious ambition to become an international virtuoso of the violin. He devoted all his youthful energies to this end in his boyhood, neglecting all else, including ordinary school work. It was never to materialise, that ambition with the violin; but it remained with him for some while and the legacy of it never seems entirely to have left him, for much of the music he subsequently wrote for the violin, including the one full-scale concerto, is full of memories of that old ambition, and perhaps even at times passing regrets for it.

He worked hard and the ambition was serious. However, like

15

many middle class families then, as now, music was not considered by the Sibelius family as a suitable or properly serious profession. He showed little academic aptitude in the conventional sense, as much from lack of interest and application as from lack of natural ability; anything outside music soon seemed to him both boring and irrelevant. But a more acceptable way of life and a more secure future were required of him: accordingly he was encouraged to pursue his musical studies solely as a pleasant sideline and diversionary activity, but obliged to apply his serious attention to matters more substantial and 'respectable'. He acquiesced to the extent of passing his examinations for entry to Helsinki University in 1885 to study law, an accepted panacea for acceptable employment in adult life. But at the same time he was allowed to enrol in the Conservatoire to continue his studies with the violin, also to take lessons in harmony and counterpoint on a part-time basis. He had begun to compose before he went to the Conservatoire and the habit had already become deeply ingrained. Inevitably, the conflict inside him assumed ominous proportions, and inevitably music overwhelmed law. Like Edward Elgar, he soon abandoned the law and gave himself over entirely to music—parental and other opposition notwithstanding.

Helsinki University.

Martin Wegelius: Sibelius's
great teacher and friend.

There are some young men who subsequently become
outstanding composers who have the great good fortune to come
under the influence of exactly the right teacher at exactly the right
time. One remembers Beethoven and Christian Gottlob Neefe,
Brahms and Eduard Marxsen, Delius and Thomas Ward. The
young Jean Sibelius was such a one. He had entered the
Conservatoire to study first with Mitrofan Vasilec and then with
Hermann Csillag; but fortune smiled even more beneficently on
him when the Director of the Conservatoire, Martin Wegelius,
took him in hand. Wegelius was one of those teachers who
recognise exceptional talent when they see it and have both the
tact and the ability to foster and nurture it. As so often in such
cases the teacher was neither as gifted nor as originally motivated
as the pupil; but he had precisely the qualities needed at a specific

17

time by a specific pupil. Wegelius not only restrained the young Sibelius's more intemperate aspirations (and when young Jean Sibelius was a headstrong and wilful aspirant to fame), he also imbued his pupil with the soundest possible academic principles of musical composition and provided an unassailable foundation in compositional technique that was to last him through the rest of his life. But more than that: Wegelius became not only a valued mentor but also a personal friend and confidant. Sibelius would often stay with Wegelius in his private house and generally a relationship grew between the two of them that was no less personal than it was professional.

Wegelius encouraged Sibelius to continue his studies outside Finland. The master had taught the pupil as much as he could and the time had come for a broadening of the horizons. It was at one time suggested that Sibelius should go to St Petersburg to study with Rimsky-Korsakov, himself a noted teacher of composition and at one time the teacher of Igor Stravinsky. But nothing came of that and in the end Sibelius went to study with Albert Becker in Berlin. This had a number of incidental advantages; Becker never exercised the same influence over the young Sibelius as Wegelius had and always would, but being in Berlin enabled him to hear and take part in the musical life of a major European capital and to make close acquaintance with both new music and the German classics, notably Beethoven. Even more than that, and, in retrospect, even more curious in its way was that in Berlin he met his Finnish compatriot Robert Kajanus who was there to promote his own *Aino* Symphony at a Philharmonic concert and who was to become one of his, Sibelius's, most ardent champions and interpreters later on.

An immediate result of this meeting with Kajanus was that hearing the *Aino* Symphony turned Sibelius's attention to the Finnish national epic the *Kalevala* which was to be a primary source of inspiration to him for the rest of his life.

Even before leaving for Berlin he had begun to attract a little local notice with his compositions. He had also, in 1889 which was his last year at the Conservatoire, met and become close friends with Ferruccio Busoni who had come to Helsinki as professor of piano. The two young men soon warmed to each other and found themselves in concurrent personal as well as artistic sympathy. They both learnt from each other and enjoyed the social pleasures, regularly painting the town various shades of red in a way which soon became the talk of it.

Despite all this, though, Busoni found time to become engaged to and marry a Swedish girl named Gerda Sjöstrand, and Sibelius to cultivate the family of the Finnish patriot and local administrator, General Järnefelt. The Järnefelts found Sibelius a

Sibelius in Berlin, 1889.

ROBERT KAJANUS.

543

Left:
The conductor Robert
Kajanus, one of Sibelius's first
and most ardent champions.

Right:
Ferruccio Busoni. He and
Sibelius became close friends.

lively and entertaining young fellow though his socially inferior
status at first caused some mild suspicions. However, that was
swiftly overcome and indeed he soon fell for and eventually
became engaged to the daughter Aino. With the three Järnefelt
brothers he was quickly on terms of close friendship; they were all
artistically inclined, the youngest, Armas, being the composer of
the well-known *Berceuse* and an also popular *Praeludium* as well
as other and more substantial works seldom heard today. Armas
had also studied with Martin Wegelius and went on to become an
internationally famous conductor of symphony and opera.

Young Sibelius was always a high liver. If his later reputation,
especially from his middle years, was of a stern, unyielding,
uncompromisingly austere character, most notable for unsmiling
severity, the Sibelius of youth was the total opposite. He was a
man-about-town, several towns; he drank too much, spent too
much, enjoyed dalliance (or more) with the ladies, generally
'lived it up'. After Berlin (and after he had become officially
engaged to Aino) he went to Vienna where from all accounts he
indulged himself to the full. But he did not neglect his musical
studies and activities: he continued to work hard and to pay

20

Sibelius in Vienna, 1891.

attention to his proper business. He studied with Robert Fuchs and occasionally with the composer Carl Goldmark. But whatever effort he put into his music, it did not at once come back on the waters. He was still thinking about a career as a concert violinist, and as a stepping stone to that end he auditioned for a place in the Vienna Philharmonic Orchestra. He failed. What effect that failure had upon him personally, we can only guess; but musically it probably made no difference at all. If he was still intent upon turning himself into a violin virtuoso, it seems very likely that he already realised it was a spent dream: his audition for the Vienna Philharmonic was almost certainly as much in the interests of finding a way of adding to his slender finances and subsidising his social extravagances as of advancing his cause as a concert fiddler.

If he did not achieve the status of a member of one of Europe's greatest and most prestigious orchestras, his time in Vienna was still rewarding. He came to closer and fuller understanding of Beethoven and seems, too, to have found the symphonies of Anton Bruckner considerably to his liking and, eventually, grist to his creative mill when he came into his own as a composer. The

21

matter of Wagner is less clear, more indirect. He did not pay his first visit to Bayreuth until 1948, but it is obvious that when he did hear Wagner's music dramas, especially *Tristan und Isolde* and *Parsifal*, the experience deeply affected him. On the surface his own music does not appear to have many 'Wagnerian' over- or undertones; but underneath it may be a little different. Sibelius himself was never too forthcoming about Wagner's effect on him; it is even possible, perhaps likely, that he had been more moved than he cared to admit at Bayreuth and tended ever afterwards to cover his tracks and set up a kind of defensive barrier against a ghost that haunted him too much. No doubt Sibelius was also influenced by Martin Wegelius who had been an ardent Wagnerian. Sibelius's own musical creativity did not develop along Wagnerian lines, though in one sense there were apparent affinities: Sibelius drew potently upon northern myth and saga, though the source was somewhat different from Wagner's; also, he developed a method of vocal writing that had he turned his hand to music drama might well have paralleled that of Wagner, though again in a different style and manner.

That, however, can be left for later. For the moment it is adequate to note the fact and leave the conclusions until his own

The celebrated composer Carl Goldmark: Sibelius occasionally studied with him in Vienna.

ARMAS JÄRNEFELT.

Aino Järnefelt, later Aino Sibelius. Daughter of local administrator General Järnefelt.

Left:
Armas Järnefelt, brother of Aino and therefore Sibelius's brother-in-law. Became famous as composer and conductor.

unique manner of composition had settled and resolved itself on its own terms. In the immediate context it is enough to follow through his early development as a composer without speculating upon wider conclusions.

His orchestral style—and that is what currently matters—was by no means fully formed. He wrote an Overture in E major, passed it to Goldmark for criticism and had the satisfaction of hearing it performed by Robert Kajanus in Helsinki later on. He wrote some chamber music which has not survived and some songs which earned Brahms's tentative approval. He had at one time hoped to study with Brahms in Vienna; he went armed with a letter of introduction, but it does not seem to have done him

23

much good. That in itself was hardly surprising: Brahms was notorious for not encouraging young hopefuls who came to him with letters of introduction.

For the time being Sibelius continued to enjoy life and make the best of what good fortune lay in his path. But that was only on the surface: underneath there was much brewing. He returned to Finland in 1891 and immediately set about completing a large choral/orchestral work based on parts of the *Kalevala* which eventually emerged as what became known as the *Kullervo* Symphony, the first of his major works to see the light of day. It was withdrawn after the first performances (the first of all was on 28 April 1892) and Sibelius would never again allow it to be performed during his lifetime. It was resurrected in 1958, the year after his death, and has since established itself as an integral part of his total oeuvre. It has thus assumed in retrospect a significance denied to it while he lived and was honoured as a leading figure on the international music scene. Exactly why Sibelius withdrew *Kullervo* and forcibly suppressed all attempts to revive it is not clear. Obviously he felt he had passed beyond the stage of his own evolution which it represented, but there must have been other, deeper seated reasons why he remained so adamant. From time to time later in his life he did consider returning to the score and revising it; but the temptation was always resisted. Fortunately, he did not destroy the autograph but left it to be preserved in the library of Helsinki University where it rested until it was resurrected after his death.

The story deals with the life and times, the exploits and misfortunes of Kullervo, one of the legendary figures of Finnish mythology. The crux of the matter is that Kullervo during the course of one of his adventures comes upon a beautiful maiden whom he persuades to join him on his journeyings; he seduces her—only to discover to his (and her) mortification that she is his sister. The Wagnerian element will not be missed, though the dénouement is hardly in the heroic Wagner mould; both are so struck with grief and remorse by the dreadful discovery that she, without hesitation, dies and Kullervo himself, after seeking in vain for death in battle, eventually throws himself upon his sword. In Wagner's *Ring* the incest motif is strong—and its implications are not avoided, even welcomed. But here it brings nothing but misery and disgrace. The anthropology of incest has since often been explored and examined, not least by Sigmund Freud; but in this particular context the more conventional and traditional view not surprisingly prevailed. That, however, applies to the matter of the story and the drama, not to the music Sibelius brought to it. If the subject has neo-Wagnerian overtones there is little suggestion of it in the music. If there is a direct musical inheritance it is mostly Russian, specifically Tchaikovskian. It can easily be demonstrated that as a musician Sibelius grew out of the Russians (though he did not stay there long); indeed, he himself once said of Tchaikovsky, 'There is a lot of that man in me.' The Tchaikovskian influences in Sibelius have often been overplayed, especially in performances of the earlier works; but there is no denying their deeper lying incidence. The overt Tchaikovskyisms are particularly noticeable in the second movement of *Kullervo*, headed 'Kullervo's Youth' and, like the introductory movement, is purely orchestral. But the Russian inheritance is there all through. On the other hand, and especially in the vocal writing of the central section, 'Kullervo and His Sister', there is a dark, rock-like quality which speaks eloquently of the Sibelius to come and strikes a new and individual note.

The première of *Kullervo* soon after Sibelius's return to Finland from Vienna was a notable success and virtually established his reputation. This had two important consequences: first it enabled him to marry Aino Järnefelt, on 10 June 1892; secondly, it confirmed in him his determination to continue composing and to complete other major works either already on the stocks or formulating in his mind. Thus *Kullervo* had its twofold significance in Sibelius's life even though part of that significance was not fully revealed until after his death.

'Maxmo', the Tottesund manor house where Sibelius and Aino Järnefelt were married on 10 June 1892.

25

After his return from Vienna and its manifold enticements and diversions, Sibelius at first found it hard to settle to serious work. *Kullervo* progressed 'very slowly'. As it progressed he was able to pause from time to time to take stock. In a letter to Aino the previous December he had written in a mood of realistic self-criticism:

There are many things in the introduction to *Kullervo* into which I have put my whole heart and soul but there are others which aren't so good. The climax tells how Kullervo journeys by sledge to see his sister to whom he makes love. I thought of portraying this by a broad melody, some hundred bars or so, on the violins, violas and cellos in unison, with some rhythmic by-play in the lower brass. The whole climax is more powerful than anything I have ever done before . . .

After the first allegro I think one wants a pastoral mood by way of contrast. It would be a more musical solution . . .

There is more in the same vein; in fact a detailed account of the work's progress exists and has been published, but the important point is that when Sibelius himself premièred *Kullervo* it was a huge success and marked the real beginning of his climb to both national and international fame.

After honeymooning with Aino in Karelia, Sibelius took up two teaching appointments* in Helsinki and continued to work on his compositions. The appointments, both part-time, were with Robert Kajanus's conducting academy and at the Conservatoire under Martin Wegelius; the most important of his contemporary compositions was what was destined to become the first of his nationally flavoured tone poems and one of the most enduringly popular. Deeply impressed by the success of *Kullervo* Kajanus at once commissioned an orchestral work to follow it. The result was *En Saga* which Sibelius himself premièred, on 16 February 1893.

In a number of respects the whole of Sibelius's life and career could be described as 'En Saga' (A Saga). There is no specific programme, but the whole is infused with the spirit of national myth and legend. It was not, however, a marked success, as *Kullervo* had been, and in this sense it was a disappointment to Kajanus, to the audience, and no less to Sibelius himself. What exactly Kajanus and the Finnish audience did expect we can only guess at, but whatever it was they seemed not to have got it. Yet listening today, one cannot help wondering: *En Saga* has all the fervour and flavour that was to distinguish the name of Jean Sibelius strongly marked and stamped on it. The tone of voice is

---

*'Never pay attention to what critics say,' he warned a pupil. 'Remember,' he said, 'a statue has never been set up in honour of a critic!'

unmistakable. It was unmistakable from the very first bars in *Kullervo*; it was stronger rather than weaker in *En Saga*. Perhaps the lack of a vocal text or a narrative programme left the audience with no strong focal points to fix on. Whatever it was, *En Saga* did not please and was quickly withdrawn for revision. And perhaps that provides a small clue. The revised version, considerably tightened and structurally strengthened and the one we always hear today, did not appear until 1901, by which time Sibelius's confidence and technical aplomb had increased immeasurably. The original score was over-long, too diffuse and weakly constructed. In the revision these faults were in good part corrected so that the melodic freedom and the richness of tonality, musically the distinguishing features of the work and those which were most authentically 'Sibelian' were reinforced. But if the revised version had been produced first, would it have enjoyed greater success? Almost certainly not: the new voice which Sibelius brought into music needed time to become assimilated, not least in his own country and among his fellow countrymen whom he addressed most directly and most immediately.

Jean Sibelius never was and never aspired to be an opera composer. Whether he had been 'warned off' involvement in opera, or music drama, or whether his creative constitution was simply not attuned to it, it was not a field he elected to plough. Perhaps his experience of Richard Wagner and Bayreuth had worked inside him to avoid operatic temptations. Either way, opera/music drama does not feature in Sibelius's catalogue and does not seem to have ever moved seriously in his direction. All the same, his next venture was in that very direction. In retrospect, it is perhaps hardly surprising that the mission was abortive. As was his habit for most of his life, beginning with *Kullervo*, he turned for his theme to the *Kalevala*. This time the subject was *The Building of the Boat (Veneen luomimen)*, taken from Runos XVI-XVII which, in fact, relate a sequel to the story that was to furnish Sibelius with the programme for one of his later and famous symphonic tone poems, *Pohjola's Daughter*. The initial suggestions for the opera came from the literator J. J. Erkko* who urged a co-operation on the project between himself and Sibelius. Sibelius set to work with apparently some enthusiasm, made preliminary sketches, attended to the libretto, and generally seemed fired with ambitions not only to build the

---

*I believe that music alone — that is to say, absolute music — cannot by itself satisfy.

Sibelius, in a Letter to J.J. Erkko 1893

boat but also to launch it. But the fire and the enthusiasm soon began to die down and he realised that opera was not for him. Nothing remains of the project now, with one exception, and that an important one. The one surviving excerpt is the orchestral number that was originally planned as the Prelude, and has been known ever since as *The Swan of Tuonela*. This magically evocative and entirely original piece was to be incorporated as No. 3 of the Four Legends which Sibelius issued as his Op. 22 in 1895-6.

Already the pattern of Sibelius's life and work was beginning to emerge with some clarity. The course was set: it had still to be worked out in some of its finer details and the essence distilled into a purer form as the process of maturing that lies behind and beneath every life and all creative activity continued; but already the main points of the compass were charted, so to speak. Thereafter was to be a steady evolution and firm growth from fundamental premises already established. What was to come was prepared for, even if it could not be fully anticipated if only because the unfolding and maturing of genius does not proceed along predictable and foreseen (or foreseeable) lines but pilots its own autonomous course.

In the extra-musical as well as the musical sense this remains true. Jean Sibelius was involved in the life and times around him. If in his later years he seemed to be something of a recluse and a spectator of rather than a participant in the busy scene of the first half of the twentieth century, the appearance in fact belies the reality. Certainly he was never a merely passive spectator. He maintained a lively interest in what went on around him; events and happenings both musical and non-musical attracted his attention. It could not in the non-musical sense at any rate be avoided: he lived in a part of the world where history as well as climate struck hard and with often lethal intentions and he could not, nor did he wish to, avoid or evade it. Indeed, in his youth especially he deliberately involved himself in the affairs and aspirations of his nation and his century.

A portrait of the young Sibelius as he was at the time when he was still a student under Martin Wegelius has come down to us from the pen of the leading Finnish critic of the day, Carl Flodin, who clearly was impressed. It is worth quoting because it illuminates aspects of his youthful personality that may seem at some odds with the later impressions:

There was something strangely winning about his slender figure. It was as if his upright, straightforward nature always wanted to meet one with open arms. Yet you were still not quite sure whether there was not some secret leg-pulling behind it all. His conversation overflowed with

Carl Flodin, the leading Finnish musical critic who wrote a perceptive piece on the young Sibelius.

paradoxical statements and ideas without one being able to say how much was serious and how much simply played on the surface, like bubbles of notions and passing whimsies generated in his fertile brain. His fair hair fell in disorder onto his forehead. His eyes had a veiled expression, but when his restless imagination began to work, they became more penetrating and took on a bluish shimmer. His ears were remarkable—large, well-shaped 'sound receivers', the ears of a musician such as Beethoven must have had . . .

Aspects of Finland

Opposite page
Above:
Latvajävi.
Stahlberg.

Below:
Uhtuan Lamminophja.
L. K. Inha.

Right:
Nilsiá.
L. K. Inha.

Below:
Gard (Kiestingistá).
Stahlberg

Above:
Norra Esplanadgatan,
Helsinki.
Daniel Nyblin

Right:
Eno.
L. K. Inha.

Chapter 2

The Patriot

All his life Sibelius was a fervent patriot, but in his early years it was true in a particular sense. During the 1890s, when Sibelius's first manhood was emerging, Finland was dominated by Tsarist Russia and, as in so many cases in the late nineteenth century, strongly nationalistic feelings and movements were rising. Sibelius vigorously supported such movements and through his music gave conscious expression to those feelings. He associated with a number of writers who were active in the cause of Finnish independence, including his brother-in-law Arvid Järnefelt, and was a leading supporter of both their cause and their newspaper, *Päivälehti*. Indeed, by marrying into the Järnefelt family, one of the leading Finnish speaking families, he had outwardly allied himself with Finnish nationalism as well as increasing his social status.

One of the first musical results of Sibelius's nationalistic leanings and sympathies and the public recognition of them was a commission from the Viipuri Students Association for some music to go with a series of historical tableaux. For this purpose he virtually abandoned work on his opera and produced during the middle months of the year an overture and a suite of three orchestral pieces which bore the name *Karelia*. The once popular overture has more or less disappeared from circulation but the suite, consisting of the Intermezzo, Ballad and Alla Marcia, became and has remained one of his most genuinely popular (in the sense of reaching beyond the generally interested musical audience) and most frequently performed works.

More important than this however, from both points of view, was the next major composition to come from him. 'Major work' might perhaps be taken as a mildly invidious term in the circumstance. The 'Four Legends', or 'Lemminkäinen Suite' as it is sometimes referred to, arose in part out of the ideas and sketches for the abandoned opera project *The Building of the Boat*.

Although the projected Prelude was the only part of the music to have survived substantially intact, as *The Swan of Tuonela*, some of the other ideas were later moulded into the Legends. This is most specifically true of the fourth number, known variously as 'Lemminkäinen's Homecoming', 'Lemminkäinen's Return', or 'Lemminkäinen's Homeward Journey'. But in fact the whole of the 'Lemminkäinen Suite' owes its origins to the motive force that went into the original conception of the opera.

The 'Legends', or 'Suite', has a curious history. The most celebrated number, *The Swan of Tuonela*, abides no question. The imaginative implication is quite clear and overt: Tuonela, the land of death, the hell of Finnish mythology, is surrounded by a large river with black waters and a rapid current, on which the Swan of Tuonela floats majestically, singing.

Musically the piece is even more remarkable; indeed, it may justly be called the first wholly original piece Sibelius wrote and the one that gives the first complete clues to the internal secret of his true originality. It is not too much to say that without a proper understanding of the musical implications of *The Swan of Tuonela* it is impossible to come to grips fully with the essential musical quality of his later compositions.

The first and perhaps most significant feature of *The Swan of Tuonela* is its melodic structure, specifically the long winding asymmetric melody given to the *cor anglais* as the swan sings its melancholy song of death. This way of laying out a melody was to become typical of Sibelius's practice and one of his most distinguishing features. It pervades, either in fact or by implication, much of his subsequent music. It may be seen as his individual response to the late nineteenth-century/romantic search for ways to free music from the domination of classical music by formal terminal melody—what Wagner was seeking through what he called 'unending *melos*' and Debussy meant when he said: 'We want free speech in music, infinite melody, infinite variation, and freedom of musical phrase.' It was therefore something not in general terms particular to Sibelius but in accord with a general feeling towards a fresh approach to melodic construction. (Beethoven had already been working towards something like it in his last quartets and sonatas.)

The other notable feature of *The Swan* is harmonic-modal flavour which also became more and more characteristic of Sibelius's music, reaching its overt peak in the Sixth Symphony. Both these aspects will emerge in greater clarity and greater detail as the story of his life and (musical) times unfolds.

The other two 'Legends' have found less favour independently. The first, 'Lemminkäinen and the Maidens of Saari', was not finalised until 1937 and the second, 'Lemminkäinen in Tuonela'

Press Celebration Days 1899 from Hufvudstadsbladet 4 November 1899 containing the programme which included the Tableau 'Finland Awakes', which later became *Finlandia*.

was not published for many years. The former is the most backward looking of the set, with its overtones of Slavonic romanticism, though it is evocative in its way and very Scandinavian in atmosphere. It 'tells' how Lemminkäinen pursues the beautiful Kyllikki into the land of Saari, finds her unresponsive and consoles himself with the Maidens and the dancing and festivities. The latter, 'Lemminkäinen in Tuonela', is more ominous. In it Lemminkäinen is killed by a herdsman from Pohjola just as he is about to shoot the Black Swan with a crossbow and his body is borne to Tuonela on the dark waters of death. This, however, is all based on myth and legend and things do not follow their natural courses (it is again based on Runos from the *Kalevala*), and the victim's dismembered body is sewn together by his mother's magic, he is released from Tuonela and rides headlong homewards to music of, again, great power and originality, the trochaic meter (long short/long short stresses) evoking the headlong ride in a way that was to become another typically Sibelian musical hallmark.

Late in his life Sibelius looked back in affection to the 'Legends' and considered them worthy to stand beside his symphonies, though there is no suggestion that they in any meaningful sense add up to something like the four movements of a symphony proper. He was right; these four pieces revolving round the figure of a typical Nordic hero contain not only some of his own most remarkable early music but some of the most original and individual music written anywhere at the time. All of which makes it the more surprising that Sibelius should have had serious doubts (in one case supported by Robert Kajanus*) about two of the numbers which caused him to withhold them for so long.

In one way things did not go so well for him on the personal plane. He had long coveted the position of Music Director at Helsinki University, and in 1896 he made a strong application for it. This brought him into direct confrontation with Kajanus and caused some bad feeling and perpetrated animosity. This was not healthy or helpful: Kajanus had always been one of Sibelius's leading champions, and when Sibelius was elected the terms were so inimical in Kajanus's view that he felt compelled to protest and appeal the following year. The decision in Kajanus's favour did nothing to calm the troubled waters and the schism in the two men's friendship lasted for some while, though happily it was later resolved and Kajanus again became the foremost interpreter and champion of Sibelius and his music (Kajanus made some of the first and most authoritative recordings of Sibelius which did an enormous amount to spread the gospel of Sibelius outside Finland and were sponsored by the Finnish government).

A happier outcome of this temporary dissension was that it appears to have borne directly upon the decision of the Finnish authorities to grant Sibelius a life pension to enable him to reduce his teaching commitments and concentrate on his composing. This enlightened move was unique among supposedly civilised governments. (Earlier composers, including, perhaps

---

*The conductor Kajanus, one of Sibelius's most intimate friends, sought to excuse himself [after dinner] and take his departure, as he was due to conduct a concert at Petrograd next day. The others present protested that the occasion was not one to be sacrificed to such sordid material considerations, and pressed Kajanus to telephone through to Petrograd and cancel the engagement. Seeming to comply with the suggestion, Kajanus left the table, but went to the station, took train to Petrograd, conducted the concert, and returned to Helsinki, where, on re-entering the restaurant, he found the company still seated at the same table, engaged in the same animated discussion. On seeing him, Sibelius mildly expostulated with him, saying, 'That was surely a very long telephone call of yours, Kajanus!'

primarily, Beethoven, received pensions to this end from aristocracy and wealthy patrons, but for the most part governments have remained indifferent when not actually hostile). The pension awarded was hardly such as to bestow true wealth on its recipient, but it was sufficient to keep head above water. On the other hand, Sibelius's habits of high living and high spending were still uncurbed and continued to be so for many years, in fact in one form or another for the rest of his life, despite frequent bouts of impecunity. In one sense, however, the limited amount of the pension was an advantage: it was sufficient to keep the wolf from the door and lift the most undermining pressures off him, but not sufficient to enable him to live out his life in idle extravagance. He would probably never have done so; he would have continued to compose out of inner necessity even more than public duty, but the award did show a nice sense of judgment and preserved a judicious balance between useful practicality and wicked temptation.

Finnish nationalism was by now gathering added momentum and in the process was drawing Sibelius deeper into its machinations. And inevitably it brought repressive measures in its wake—which no less inevitably served only to feed its fires. There was something called the 'February Manifesto', issued by the Russian authorities and twisting the screw a turn further on Finnish aspirations. The musical upshot of all this on Sibelius's part was a rush of patriotic music. The most significant work in this genre came with a series of tableaux ostensibly mounted to celebrate the doings of the Press Pension Fund but in fact a strongly motivated patriotic demonstration. This took place in 1899 and contained music subsequently published as the first set of *Scènes historiques,* Op.25 and a finale called 'Finland Awakes' which after quick revision became the piece that has ever since been known as *Finlandia* and the one which spells the name of Jean Sibelius to the world at large.

Immediately before these political preoccupations Sibelius had written the first of his several contributions to the theatre, not in the field of opera or music drama but in that of incidental music, a rôle he undertook virtually to the end of his composing career and one which appears to have particularly suited him. He was always interested in the theatre: indeed, his interest and occasional participation was such that it remains something of a mystery that, with one exception, his operatic ventures proved to be either abortive or non-existent. This is the more surprising because he was still quite young when he declared that music only fulfils itself totally in conjunction with words. This echoes Mahler's concept as 'the word as bearer of the idea' and several of Wagner's contentions and conclusions. But for Sibelius it never

Adolf Paul, author of the play *King Christian II* for which Sibelius provided incidental music.

became so, at least in practical terms. Although he made his notable musical contributions to the theatre and composed a number of non-theatrical vocal works of quality—for instance, the original and beautiful *Luonnotar*—his dramatic music remained squarely in the realm of incidental music. His last completed major work was his music for a production of Shakespeare's *The Tempest* in Copenhagen in 1926.

His first excursion into this field came in 1898 when he wrote a substantial score for Adolf Paul's play *King Christian II*. This drama, very successful at the time, concerns the love of King

Sibelius in 1900.

Christian, sovereign over three countries, Denmark, Norway and Sweden, for a lowly Dutch girl, Dyveke, who ends as a victim of murder. For the original production Sibelius contributed only four items but added some further ones later. This music is in early Sibelius's best light style and scored for modest forces, in part because orchestral and instrumental resources in Finland were at that time minimal. According to Sibelius himself there were only two bassoon players available and one of them was consumptive! (Hence the scoring to the famous 'Musette' which calls for two bassoons and two clarinets although according to Sibelius 'it should be for bagpipes and reeds'.)

All the music is delightful and is still performed frequently, although the play itself has long since disappeared from circulation. Apparently, though, Sibelius did not think a great deal of it, for when Hans Winderstein conducted it in Leipzig, its composer said that 'it has embarrassed me' since it is 'salon music . . . it is not intended as a piece to introduce me abroad. I have the greatest ambition to stand before you as a composer for whom you can have some regard'—this in a letter to Busoni.

The 'some regard' he hoped to establish with a symphony which was currently occupying his mind. He had for some time been convinced that a full-scale orchestral symphony was needed from him. He accordingly worked upon it during 1898-9 and his First Symphony, in E minor, Op.39 was presented, under Sibelius's own direction, on 28 April 1899. It was well received and it virtually determined the future course of his composing career. The note struck was heroic, and if it was not overtly patriotic and nationalistic, in many senses it was so by indirect implication. It also exposed some typically Sibelian musical features among others that appear, at least in retrospect, as fairly straightforward and conventional. The originality is stamped on its very first bars, the long clarinet solo, at first over a soft drum roll, in its latter part unaccompanied. This is of great importance. Firstly it has the kind of asymmetrical melodic structure that Sibelius first deployed in *The Swan of Tuonela*; secondly, it contains the melodic germs of much that is to follow and anticipates his remark to Gustav Mahler,* during their famous meeting in Helsinki in 1907, that what attracted him about the symphony was its severity of style and the logic which led to the close interconnection of all the motifs.

In many respects the First Symphony stands on the hinge between the receding nineteenth and the coming twentieth centuries. Much of it has unmistakable Slavonic overtones, notably in its principal themes; on the other hand much of the subsidiary material echoes Finnish material. This creates a kind of dramatic tension which might be seen to parallel Finland's struggle for independence against Russian domination and oppression. Looking back to Sibelius's remark about Tchaikovsky it could be said that 'there is a lot of that man in this symphony'. But not too much: even though it is the most 'romantic' and opulent of Sibelius's symphonies, too much indulgence in performance leads to emotional and aesthetic distortion. If some of the themes, especially that in the finale, sound like the kind of big round pot-bellied tune so beloved of the nineteenth-century romantics, that is not the true Sibelius note and tone: a harder, tougher-minded logic and motivation is

---

*In November 1907, while on a conducting visit to Finland, a definitive dialogue on the nature of the symphony took place between Mahler and Sibelius. 'Mahler's grave heart trouble forced him to lead an ascetic life, and he was not fond of dinners and banquets. Contact was established between us in some walks,' recalled Sibelius. 'When our conversation touched on the essence of the symphony, I said that I admired its severity and style and the profound logic that created an inner connection between all the motifs . . .

'Mahler's opinion was just the reverse, *"Nein, die Symphonie muss sein wie die Welt. Sie muss alles umfassen."* [No, the symphony must be like the world. It must embrace everything]

required. This symphony, for all its external luxuriance, contains that hard core of intellectual force and uncompromising integrity that more and more came to characterise Sibelius's music. Just as if you strip away the decorations and pianistic virtuosities of much of Liszt's earlier piano music the austere and economical style of his later pieces can be discerned underneath, so with Sibelius's earlier music, this symphony perhaps especially, if the outer opulence is stripped away the uncompromising lines of the later Sibelius are revealed.

All this applies primarily to the first and most original of the symphony's four movements; but it does have more or less direct relevance all through. And it is important, because the First Symphony launched the series on which, more than any other, Sibelius's reputation and standing in the light of musical history rests.

Axel Carpelan, Sibelius's friend and champion who encouraged him to work on his Second Symphony.

The second movement, Andante, has the elements of a folk song (whether or not it is actually derived from one has been argued without conclusion); the scherzo is clearly derived from the corresponding movement of the Beethoven Ninth with its powerful drum motif; and the Finale, marked 'Quasi una fantasia', has its big romantic tune but also some anticipation of the more mature Sibelius to come.

Sibelius's reputation outside Finland needed a while to establish itself, but it soon took root in Germany where his music was not only performed and appreciated but also published by Breitkopf & Härtel who became from then on his European publishers until the outbreak of the First World War put an end to all his German connections. In 1900 he accompanied Kajanus and the Finnish Orchestra on a tour through Scandinavia and on to the Paris World Exhibition where Mahler and the Vienna Philharmonic also appeared, though with rather less success. (The failure of Mahler and the Viennese orchestra to make the desired impression was instrumental in still further weakening Mahler's position as conductor and music director which was soon to lead to his resignation.)

For the Finnish contingent however the visit and the tour were a marked success. Sibelius conducted some of his own pieces and the reception accorded to them encouraged him to begin serious work on a new symphony which had been gestating in his creative imagination for some time. Like Brahms and Beethoven (and one or two others) before him, Sibelius had waited to gain experience of both art and life before embarking on the difficult and demanding task of composing a full-scale orchestral symphony. But having taken the first hurdle and successfully presented his opening gambit in that field of endeavour, he did not waste time in following it up with a second. His friend and champion Axel Carpelan persuaded him that he should go to Italy, a country he already knew and loved, in order to free himself from teaching and other distractions in Helsinki and concentrate on his symphony. Carpelan also took the lead in raising funds from wellwishers to help advance the project. In the event Sibelius made his way to Italy by way of Germany, where he dallied awhile at Leipzig and made contact with Artur Nikisch, the outstanding conductor.

But it did not work out quite as Carpelan and his backers originally intended. In Italy, instead of settling quietly to work on the symphony, he moved around meeting people and turning over a number of other things and projects in his mind, including a symphony on the subject of Dante and some musings on Don Juan. The original plan did not, however, misfire. The symphony thrust itself to the working top of his mind and gradually reduced all other ideas to ultimate irrelevance. He returned home to Finland via Prague where he renewed acquaintance with Suk and found a sympathetic figure in Antonin Dvořák, and by the end of the year, 1901, the symphony was nearly ready. It would have been quite ready had not Sibelius, true to his own strong and growing sense of self-criticism, remained for a long time dissatisfied with some aspects of it. More than once the projected première was postponed but eventually took place on 8 March 1902.

It, too, was a success. It has become Sibelius's most popular and most performed symphony, though it has also become the one most easily and avidly turned on by hostile critics, largely because it has more of the true Sibelian characteristics than the earlier one but still retains overhangs of what came to be regarded as unacceptable elements of romantic rhetorical excess. Thus as early as 1940, long before the 'reaction' against Sibelius set in and while in many areas his reputation was still at its peak, often exaggerated by over-extravagant praise, Virgil Thomson in the *New York Herald Tribune* dismissed the Second Symphony as:

Vulgar, self-indulgent, and provincial beyond description.

This may have been a foretaste of a widely-held view among professional musicians later, but it certainly was not so during, say, the 1930s, when Sibelius's star had risen and was in the ascendant in England and America as well as in Scandinavia. Indeed, much of the charge against Sibelius was directed at precisely those elements in his style that he was busy working out of his system in the first three symphonies.

As in the First Symphony, the most original material of the Second lies in the first movement. If the opening suggests a kind of Brahms transmogrified—and not only in the matter of key: both Brahms and Sibelius chose D major for their second attempts at orchestral symphony—the continuation is not like Brahms at all. Hear the opening bars and the horn calls, and then we move into another world altogether. The structure is highly original; so original that some critics saw it as a total revolution. Cecil Gray, in a famous monograph first published in 1931 and an early example of the kind of eulogistic writing that in those days boosted Sibelius's reputation and later encouraged the 'reaction', after noting that the Second Symphony 'in outward appearance . . . still conforms to the traditional four-movement formula of *allegro, andante, scherzo* and *finale*', went on to say:

. . . but the organisation of the movements reveals many important innovations, amounting at times and particularly in the first movement, to a veritable revolution, and to the introduction of an entirely new principle into symphonic form . . .

Nothing in the entire literature of symphonic form is more remarkable than the way in which Sibelius here presents a handful of seemingly disconnected and meaningless scraps of melody, and then breathes life into them, bringing them into organic relation with each other and causing them to grow in stature and significance with each successive appearance, like living things.

True enough; but this is also the kind of hyperbole which in the end did Sibelius's reputation rather more harm than good. While what Gray says is not to be denied in general terms, it does fail to take into account the way certain other composers, notably Alexander Borodin, had been working towards similar procedures some forty years earlier. In Gray's favour it must be admitted that he did lay a finger on what was to become one of the salient points of Sibelius's later symphonic style—that of building symphonic movements out of tiny nuclei of themes and combining them to create structural growth. This was more or less in direct opposition to the then contemporary practice of beginning with large melodic statements and subsidiary themes arbitrarily thrown together and dignified with the name 'symphony'. In this respect, however much of Tchaikovsky there may have been in Jean Sibelius, the latter's symphonic principles were not only in direct contrast to those of Tchaikovsky but in active opposition to them. Tchaikovsky, whose symphonies tended to be arbitrary in form at least until the last, the *Pathétique*, once confessed, referring to his own Fourth Symphony, that 'the succeeding episodes were loosely held together and seams were always visible'. Whatever else may be visible in the symphonies of Sibelius, it is not the seams. The influence of Borodin must not be overlooked or undervalued; Borodin was a chemist by profession and like so many Russians essentially an amateur composer, so perhaps his insight into organic structures in nature through his chemistry gave him a particular insight which he began to translate into music and Sibelius carried on and further refined.

Because it came to characterise Sibelius's principles as a composer of symphonies and symphonic tone poems, this mild technical diversion is necessary to a proper understanding of his compositions. The slow movement and the scherzo of the Second Symphony mark a considerable advance over those in the First. The scherzo has that famous repeated note theme for the oboe in the trio—and that too is a Sibelius characteristic: repeated note motifs often appear in his works in one form or another, as in the fanfare motif of *Finlandia*. However, the main criticism of

Arvid Järnefelt, another of his wife's brothers and the author of the play *Kuolema* for which Sibelius wrote incidental music which contained as one of its numbers what in a revised edition was to become *Valse triste*.

Sibelius's detractors, including Virgil Thomson, is the finale. This follows straight on from the scherzo without a break (remembering perhaps a similar procedure in Beethoven's Fifth Symphony, though the transition is differently made by Sibelius). It begins with a broad melodic expansion and proceeds to develop into one of those apparently optimistic and emotionally buoyant conclusions which in the wake of a world depression, one world war and the onslaught of another, had come to seem wholly untenable. This was due in part to a misconception of Sibelius's motives in writing as he did. For long it was taken that this burgeoning finale (it is not all burgeoning but that could be conveniently overlooked) was another expression of Sibelius's national pride and a further declaration of Finland's aspirations towards full independence. At one level this is probably true; the whole movement carries an outward note of confident assertion and pride as it sweeps irresistibly forward on great waves of string and brass tone. But beneath the surface all is not confidence and assertion. Subsequent research has exposed much to redress the balance, and Sibelius's later commentator, Erik Tawastsjerna, has not only dispelled to a large extent the overt nationalistic pomp and circumstance which at one time was taken as a musical pamphlet of protest, even by some of Sibelius's champions inside Finland—including Robert Kajanus—but also confirmed that one theme for the woodwind was directly connected with his feelings in the aftermath of the suicide of his sister-in-law Elli Järnefelt. So the nonsense may be allowed to subside; indeed it has subsided long since in conjunction with the more unintelligent aspects of the 'reaction'.

The Second Symphony gave Sibelius one of his greatest successes. It drew packed audiences to its early performances and it has since become one of the most generally popular of all his compositions and certainly his most frequently performed symphony. Despite the false association with the cruder forms of nationalism and, what seemed at the time and in the later circumstances, somewhat blatant optimism, out of tune with the inter-war period, the Second Symphony did strike a chord in Finnish hearts and in another sense did sound a refreshing note in an age which, in the wake of worldwide disasters, became full of

Left:
Governor-General Bobrikoff, who headed the oppressive régime under Tsar Nicholas II.

Right:
Tsar Nicholas II.

cynicism and pessimism, real or simulated, justified or merely cultivated.

In the year which followed the production of the Second Symphony,* Sibelius made one of the biggest blunders, miscalculations anyway, of his life and one which he was to regret ever afterwards. In 1903 he wrote some incidental music for a play, *Kuolema*, by his brother-in-law Arvid Järnefelt. This contained music that in a revised form became the famous *Valse triste*, which he sold outright to a local publisher for a paltry sum and so denied himself a virtual fortune in royalties as it travelled all round the world in all manner of arrangements and transubstantiations. Never with money to spare, and always extravagant in his life style, *Valse triste* could have made all the difference, could have provided him with most welcome funds all through the years ahead. But he got it wrong and lived to lament it at leisure. That he was certainly not the first and will not be the last author/composer/artist to let a best seller slip through his fingers was not much compensation.

By the turn of the century Finland was enduring a surfeit of Russian oppression. Ever since the assassination of Tsar Alexander II in 1881 the situation had been deteriorating. Finland had been created a virtually autonomous Grand Duchy by Alexander I in 1809 immediately after the Treaty of Hamina (Fredrikshamn) had ended some six hundred years of virtual Swedish hegemony when Russia, incited by Napoleon, had attacked and defeated the 'Swedo-Finnish' setup in 1808. There was always feeling for and against Russian domination inside Finland; but after the assassination of Alexander II, a most moderate and sympathetic monarch who to this day is honoured in Finland, Russian oppression grew and fed Finnish nationalism. Alexander II's successor, Alexander III, along with his Danish consort, made efforts, largely against the run of Russian officialdom, to preserve Finland's autonomy, but the succession of Tsar Nicholas II in 1894 heralded a new era of restriction and oppression culminating in the régime of Governor-General Bobrikov. Even under the liberal Alexanders Finnish nationalism flowered and began to flourish. Its centre of activity was the University of Turku where the supporters were known as the Fennomen and where one of the student leaders, Johann Vilhelm Snellman, was active in demanding official recognition of the Finnish language in education and affairs.

---

*Once, while Kajanus was rehearsing the Second Symphony with only two trumpets — the third having succumbed to influenza — Sibelius interrupted him and departed abruptly. 'I can only hear the trumpet which isn't there,' he explained, 'and I can't stand it any longer.'

J. V. Snellman, a leader of
Finnish nationalism.

Caught between Sweden and Russia and longing for total
independence, Finland has had a stormy history. Swedish as well
as Finnish was, and is, the common language, even though the
most ardent patriots have argued strongly and actively in favour
of the latter and even though in many quarters Finnish was for
long regarded as the predominantly peasant language, Swedish
being preferred by the educated classes. (Sibelius himself was
born into a Swedish-speaking family.) What became the rallying
cry for Finnish patriotic nationalism was raised by Snellman who
proclaimed: 'Swedes we are no longer, Russians we cannot
become; we must be Finns.'

All this helped feed Jean Sibelius's innate patriotism and

Elias Lönnrot, who gathered together the folk tales which make up the *Kalevala*.

national fervour and encouraged him to give direct expression to it through and in his music. The feeling was particularly strong in the last years of the nineteenth century and the early years of the twentieth, precisely the years of Sibelius's rise to manhood and creative maturity. Small wonder then that he became, as much by natural right as by conscious effort, the musical spokesman for emergent Finland.

The *Kalevala* is in essence a vast collection of folk tales passed down verbally from generation to generation which were gathered together, largely in Karelia, by Elias Lönnrot and published in a single large volume by him in 1835. This was the source of so much of Sibelius's inspiration from his earliest days. He was fortunate in that although his family was Swedish-speaking he learnt the Finnish language at school and so was able to read the *Kalevala* in the original with the octosyllabic style (somewhat reminiscent of Longfellow) of the Karelian reciters and storytellers which Lönnrot preserved. Sibelius's addiction to the *Kalevala* and the inspiration he drew from it is analogous to Mahler's constant drawing on *Des Knaben Wunderhorn*, though from rather different premises since Mahler's inspiration was not primarily nationalistic.

Russian oppression of Finland continued virtually until the collapse of the Tsarist régime and the Revolution in 1917, despite a small interregnum immediately following the rising in Russia of 1905. But the full 1917 Revolution gave Finland a long looked-for chance to declare total independence—and a chance that was taken without hesitation. The Finnish Republic was formally declared on 6 December 1917 and was recognised by most European countries and by Russia first of all. This, as it turned out, did not end Finland's tribulations, which continued into civil war between the 'Red Guards' who supported Russia and her revolution, and the 'White Guards' who opted for full independence and traditional Finnish ways and customs. During the troubled 1920s and 1930s the Finnish Republic evolved and tried to settle down after the White Guards led by General Mannerheim and with German military support had triumphed, until the quarrel with Russia was revived by Stalin's invasion of 1939 and the heroic Finnish resistance during the early months of the Second World War won the admiration of the civilised world.

Finnish soldiers defend their border when Russia invaded Finland in the winter war of 1939-40

Chapter 3

Home and Abroad

Because of the length of his life and the manner in which, especially during his later years, he was so associated with not only a particular country but a specific place in it, the idea has often circulated that Jean Sibelius was a man who stayed at home composing his music and did very little else. There is a half-truth in this, but it is no more than a half-truth. In his youth, as we have seen, he moved around Europe, visiting places and countries, meeting people, learning and working his way in both life and art. But his peripatetic inclinations did not cease with youth: they continued well into mature life and although he tended after his sixtieth year to let the world come to him in his northern fastness—something it was always willing to do since he was a magnificent host and entertainer of welcome guests—rather than himself going out to find and meet it, the idea of the immovable object in human form does not really suit him at all, at least during his active career.

The success of the Second Symphony marked a turning point from both the personal and the professional points of view. After this his music more and more became characterised by that sense of economy and concision upon which his most lasting reputation is built. He remained a true Finnish patriot, but it no longer dominated his music in the way it had before. It became more subtle (like his music itself), more informed from within rather than promoted overtly. He put behind him the Romantic nationalism (or nationalistic Romanticism) of his first two symphonies and the compositions which were contemporary with them and replaced it with an artistic development which became increasingly in tune with the emerging twentieth century and with many of the evolutions in music taking place elsewhere in Europe.

But it did not come at once, certainly not 'overnight'. His next major work was the Violin Concerto which he wrote in 1903

Programme for a concert in Abo/Turku on 26 April 1904 with Viktor Novácek, violin, and including the Violin Concerto, *En Saga,* and the finale of the Second Symphony.

under the influence of his friend Willy Burmester. No doubt he still had in his mind memories of his early ambitions in the direction of becoming an international virtuoso of the violin. The concerto is full of evidence of a profound knowledge of, and interest in—and perhaps nostalgia for—the requirements of violin technique, and it has become one of the most popular and frequently performed works of its kind. It is not of course a 'display' piece in the old nineteenth-century virtuoso tradition as first established by Paganini and carried on by such as Vieuxtemps and Wieniawski. It has that toughness of mind and sinew, the hard centre beneath the display and the occasional indulgences, that one would expect from the mind and pen of Jean Sibelius.

The concerto did not, however, originally go quite as planned. Sibelius promised the first performance to Burmester; but he failed to deliver it on time and being as usual short of cash, and confident that a new work would alleviate the parlous situation, he gave the première, with Burmester's consent (whether reluctant or not is uncertain) to Viktor Novácek in Helsinki. But the opportunism misfired: Novácek was not man or artist enough for the undertaking and the work itself did not please. Sibelius immediately withdrew it for revision, though whether or not because it had been hurriedly put together and showed it, or because Sibelius himself was genuinely in the state of personal artistic development and still needed to feel his way, may still be a matter of conjecture. A bit of both probably. In any case, Sibelius was in the habit, which continued throughout his life, of withdrawing his original compositions and revising them, often so far as virtually to transform and re-compose them. The Violin Concerto is a prime example; the Fifth Symphony is an even more illuminating one. Also, like Beethoven, he more than once promised the first performance of a work to one person or organisation—then gave it to somebody else. In either case this was not necessarily, even probably, evidence of a form of dishonesty; it might simply be a matter of imposed expediency but, even more, one of the conditions under which an artist is obliged to work in a greedily competitive world attuned not to creative requirements but to practical economic considerations.

However that may be, Sibelius submitted the concerto to far-ranging revision, and after some further delay it was given a new 'first performance' in the form we know it today, in Berlin in October 1905 with Karl Halir as soloist and Richard Strauss, no less, conducting. It achieved a success then which it has enjoyed ever since.

These first years of the 1900s were busy and prolific ones for Sibelius. Besides the Violin Concerto he wrote the popular

Richard Strauss: he conducted the revised version of the Violin Concerto in Berlin in 1905; Karl Halir the soloist.

Romance in C for strings, a number of songs and piano pieces (including one of his most successful compositions for the piano, *Kyllikki* which links back to the Four Legends of the mid-1890s), as well as the Dance Intermezzo *Pan and Echo* (1906) and some other smaller pieces. But the main preoccupation of this period from the point of view of work in progress was the Third Symphony which he worked on between 1904 and 1907.

As well as his compositional activities his private affairs took a new and important direction. Extravagant as always and despite his State pension he continued to be deep in debt. Notwithstanding this, and on the familiar principle that the best way to deal with debts is to spend one's way out, in 1904 he

Maurice Maeterlinck, author
of *Pelléas et Mélisande*.

purchased a plot of land about thirty miles north of Helsinki and
proceeded to build, or have built for him, a house upon it. This
house he called 'Ainola' after his wife and there he and his family
lived for the rest of his life. It suited him perfectly; it was deep in
the Finnish countryside but near enough to Helsinki to permit,
even encourage, frequent visits to the capital for whatever
purpose pleased him at the moment, business or pleasure, usually
both. The place he had selected, Järvenpää, has become forever
associated with his name and his fame, as with Finland itself, and
through two World Wars was a refuge for himself and in between
times a place of pilgrimage for his friends and his growing number
of international admirers. Indeed, the name of Järvenpää has long

since become virtually synonymous with that of Jean Sibelius.

Firmly established as a man of property with a cherished domicile he may have been, but he did not at once, as it were, hole up and dig in. He continued his familiar activities and his travels. In January 1905 he went to Berlin to conduct the first German performance of the Second Symphony at one of Busoni's New Music concerts, after which he intended to undertake his first trip to England. He had received the invitation at the end of 1904 and laid his plans accordingly. But on his return from Berlin he received a commission to write incidental music for a production of Maurice Maeterlinck's play *Pelléas et Mélisande* at the Swedish Theatre in Helsinki in a Swedish translation by Bertel Cripenberg. Because of this he postponed his trip to England, though he had every intention of making it as soon as he could. The *Pelléas et Mélisande* music brought him further success and at least one of its numbers, 'At the Castle Gate', has joined pieces

Programme for the first performance of *Pelléas et Mélisande* with Sibelius's incidental music at the Swedish Theatre, 17 March 1905.

Sir Henry Wood, one of the first English musicians to take up Sibelius's cause.

like *Valse triste*, *Finlandia* and the *Karelia* Suite as spelling out the name of Sibelius to the general public.

More and more Sibelius's name and music were becoming known and recognised outside his native Finland. In Germany he was making excellent progress; in Italy (Milan) Arturo Toscanini was incorporating Sibelius in his concerts; his name was coming onto the lips of a number of English musicians and his compositions attracting their attention. Therefore a visit to England made sound sense. Already he had good reason to think he had influential English admirers.

He was not disappointed. He reached Liverpool in December 1905 where he conducted his First Symphony and some other items at a Ladies Concert of the Orchestral Society before making his way to London, where he immediately made contact with leading English musicians, including Henry Wood. Wood had given the first ever English performance of a Sibelius work when he presented the *King Christian* music at a Promenade Concert in December 1901; he also introduced the First Symphony in 1903 and by the time of Sibelius's first English visit had clearly

à mon bien cher et honoré ami Jean Sibelius

Rosa Newmarch

Rosa Newmarch.

established himself as England's leading Sibelius interpreter. He was not the only one, for Sir Granville Bantock had also conducted the First Symphony in 1905, and Hans Richter had given the English première of the Second Symphony at a Hallé concert, also in 1905.

Henry Wood's interest in Sibelius had been aroused first by Rosa Newmarch, a well-known writer on music who went to Russia in 1897, where she studied with Vladimir Stassov at the Imperial Public Library in St Petersburg, met many leading Russian musicians and became an expert on and ardent propagandist for Russian and Czech music and wrote several books on both. She also wrote two books on Sibelius with whom she enjoyed a long friendship and was responsible for innumerable programme notes for Queen's Hall concerts. She did much to promote Sibelius's cause in England and elsewhere. Henry Wood's practical advocacy, through performance, certainly encouraged English audiences and music lovers to take note of what was still to them a new voice. The *Musical Times* noted some time in 1906:

> The marked success of the two compositions (*En Saga* and *Finlandia*) can scarcely fail to create a desire to make further acquaintance with the works of Sibelius: their sanity and freshness will cause them to be very welcome.

Olin Downes, one of the most ardent 'Sibelians' among American critics.

England and Sibelius got onto excellent terms with each other from the start and the happy relationship lasted all through Sibelius's life. Although when the 'reaction' set in, especially after his death, the more fashionable and trendy English critics joined those in America seemingly intent on seeing how far they could go in denigrating him, his English public always remained among the most loyal of his supporters. It was in England that, after the original sponsoring of recordings of the first two symphonies by the Finnish Government, the most powerful efforts were made to spread the gospel of his music via recordings, notably with the formation by His Master's Voice, under the auspices of the late Walter Legge, of the Sibelius Society. In addition, several prominent English conductors besides Wood, including Sir Thomas Beecham,* Sir Malcolm Sargent, Sir John Barbirolli and later Anthony Collins, were always among his finest interpreters. And of course some English critics such as Cecil Gray and Constant Lambert, also Ernest Newman, set him high among composers not only of his own time but, by implication at least, of all time. (Ironically, it was what many felt to be the excessive and exaggerated praise of Sibelius by some of these critics, notably Gray and Lambert as well as Olin Downes in America, that fed the myopic forces of 'reaction' and in a certain sense made it inevitable.)

Sibelius not only found a warm welcome for his music in England, but no less for himself. English hospitality surpassed itself. Largely due to the generosity of Granville Bantock, in whose house he stayed, he remarked of this, the first of his English

---

*All my life when I have made gramophone records and listened to the tests, I have annoyed those around me by turning up the knob so the music is played *fortissimo*. Obviously, in my case, it is a necessity. I want to hear every note played. Although the effect may be distressing to the average ear, it is illuminating and edifying to *mine*, who am a workman in this. I don't make records for my own amusement, I make them to sell in the open market and it is my duty to see that all I have striven to do, with the orchestra, singers or choruses, comes off — with the utmost clarity if possible.

I was delighted, therefore, when seeing Sibelius last year, and taking some records of mine of his music, that he eagerly grasped them, put them on the gramophone and turned the knob up *twice* as high as I had ever done. There were about twelve or fifteen people in his large sitting room. After about three minutes I had a sense of vacuum and, looking round, I found the whole lot had vanished into the garden, and even there were holding their hands over their ears. But Sibelius was hanging over the machine itself and trying to get more and more tone out of it. I said, 'You have the same feeling about this sort of thing that I do.' He said, 'Oh yes, I want to hear everything. I want to hear every little note, every semi-quaver.'

Sir Thomas Beecham

60

Gustav Mahler: a famous
meeting and discussion with
Sibelius in Helsinki in 1907.

visits: 'I never made the acquaintance of English coinage.'

While in England he promised the first performance of the still
gestating Third Symphony to the Royal Philharmonic Society at
a concert conducted by Granville Bantock in March 1907.
However, according to his developing custom and, as with the
Violin Concerto, the score was not ready and the London
première had to be postponed for a year. In the event the actual
première took place in Helsinki under Sibelius's own direction,
though Bantock received the dedication, in gratitude no doubt for

his own warmth of friendship to the composer, also in recognition of the general English reception of himself and his music.

The Third Symphony is sometimes though quite unofficially known as 'the English Symphony', in part because of its dedication and its general English associations, in part on account of its musical character: some parts of it were likened to the fog banks that move along the English coastline. The identification seems reasonable enough, though whether Sibelius consciously intended it or not is arguable. (In view of his acute sensitivity to all natural phenomena and his striking ability to invoke them in music, it might well be so.)

Immediately after the Helsinki première of the symphony, Sibelius took it with him on a trip to St Petersburg, where it received a courteous if curious reception. One commentator described it as 'a suite in the style of Mendelssohn, full of sad melodies, depressing even to our ears'. The linking with Mendelssohn is interesting since Sibelius once said that he regarded Mozart and Mendelssohn as the supreme masters of the orchestra. And the reference to 'sad melodies' strikes an echo of his early affinities with Russian music, especially that of Tchaikovsky.

But the deeper significance of the Third Symphony does not lie with sad melodies or English fog banks, it lies within the structure of the music itself. Also in 1907 the famous meeting between Jean Sibelius and Gustav Mahler took place when the latter visited Helsinki in September. It was after this encounter that Sibelius reported:

When our conversation touched upon the symphony, I said that I admired its style and severity of form and the profound logic that created an inner connection between all the motifs—

and Mahler countered with:

No, no. The symphony must be like the world—it must contain everything.

The Third Symphony marks a new development in the direction of fulfilling Sibelius's concept of symphonic form and style. In the first two symphonies Sibelius had already staked his claim to original symphonic thinking; but in the Third he took a significant step towards tightening the structure, connecting the motifs and generally justifying what he had said to Mahler. Frequently it has been called the most 'classical' of his symphonies, even compared in directness and simplicity to the symphonies of Haydn, Mozart and the classical symphonists.

62

There is some truth in this, so long as one does not look too closely or analytically at either it or the 'classical' symphony; and it accords well with the statement Sibelius made later in his life:

The longer I live the more I see Classicism as the way of the future.

That of course begs a whole lot of questions: words such as 'classicism' and 'romanticism', like various political slogans, tend to get bandied about 'regardless of . . .', as Henry Wood used to say on any and every occasion, much to the amusement (always good-natured) of his orchestras. These words and terms invariably come out to mean more or less what the speaker wants them to mean. One would not say that such words from a man like Jean Sibelius are virtually meaningless, but it would be fair to say that what he did mean can only be accurately grasped through attention to and understanding of his musical compositions. And the Third Symphony gives one of the first insights into precisely what he intended to convey.

Structurally the Third Symphony is notable for the way in which symphonic form is foreshortened and for the manner in which two of its three movements—the second and third—perform a dual function—andante/scherzando and scherzo/finale. Beethoven had done something like this in certain of his works, but here Sibelius begins a process that is to become more and more typical of his symphonic procedure and points the way to the single movement form of the Seventh Symphony. This is not the place or context for extended technical analyses; all the same, Sibelius's life and work can only be understood and appreciated by frequent reference to his technical procedures. They are the blood and sinew of his creative personality, even more than with most composers.

That Sibelius took immense pains over the Third Symphony and gave it his deepest thought is clear from the time it took to come fully into being. As early as September 1904 he noted in a letter to a friend:

Have begun my new symphony.

It was not ready for production until February 1908. Nor was it his only preoccupation during that period: he planned an orchestral work to be called 'Luonnotar', but that did not materialise, though the name was used for later tone poem for voice and orchestra; in its stead he wrote one of the best known of his symphonic tone poems, Pohjola's Daughter, which he in fact called a 'symphonic fantasia'. Sibelius drew a clear distinction between symphony and symphonic poem. In conversation with Walter Legge in the 1930s he outlined his view of both forms, or genres. He rightly observed that:

> . . . since Beethoven's time all the so-called symphonies, except Brahms's have been symphonic poems. In many cases the composers have told us, or at least indicated, the programmes they had in mind; in others it is plain that there has been some story or landscape or set of images that the composer has set himself to illustrate. That is not my idea of a symphony. My symphonies are music conceived and worked out in terms of music and with no literary basis. I am not a literary musician. Of course it has happened that, quite unbidden, some mental image has established itself in my mind in connection with a movement I have been writing, but the germ and fertilisation of my symphonies have been purely musical. When I set out to write symphonic poems it is a different matter . . . these are suggested to me by our national poetry, but I do not pretend they are symphonies.

Left:
Bengt de Törne: Sibelius biographer.

Right:
Hjalmar Procopé: author of *Belshazzar's Feast*.

There is of course a good deal more question-begging and shifty arguing here. With Sibelius in particular, the 'germ and fertilisation' of the symphonic poems are and must be primarily musical; and the symphonies themselves came out of a consciousness profoundly aware of the spirit at least of 'our national poetry'. In any case, did not Beethoven himself say that he always had some *Bild* or 'picture' (the German term is not easily translatable into English) while he was composing? The very sound of Sibelius's orchestra tells us plainly that it comes from the North and aspects of the North. If, at least after the first two, Sibelius's symphonies are not 'national' in the old Romantic sense, are not in reality symphonic poems as he rightly said virtually all nineteenth-century 'symphonies' are, they are still imbued with a definable Finnish quality of thought, outlook and physical texture. Perhaps the essential 'Finnishness' of Sibelius's music is most tellingly revealed in a remark he made to his biographer and friend Bengt de Törne during a conversation which de Törne reproduced:

One day I mentioned the impression which always takes hold of me when returning to Finland across the Baltic, the first forebodings of our country being given us by low, reddish granite rocks emerging from the pale blue sea, solitary islands of a hard archaic beauty, inhabited by hundreds of white seagulls. And I concluded by saying that this landscape many centuries ago was the cradle of the Vikings. 'Yes,' Sibelius answered eagerly, and his eyes flashed, 'and when we see those granite rocks we know why we are able to treat the orchestra as we do!'

Therein lies the real secret of Sibelius's musical 'nationalism'. It lies in 'those granite rocks'. And this is as true of the symphonies as of the symphonic poems.

The score of *Pohjola's Daughter*, the impetus for which came, like the 'Four Legends', from the *Kalevala*, is prefaced by some lines from that epic, a literal translation of which runs:

Väinämöinen the magician while on a homeward journey, encounters the Maid of Pohjola, the North Country, seated on a rainbow. Overwhelmed by her beauty, he beseeches her to descend and join him, which she promises to do, if he can perform various magic feats for her. The last of these, to make a boat for her out of the fragments of her spindle, is too much for him. He has to give up in despair. Louhi's daughter remains on her rainbow, and Väinämöinen jumps back onto his sleigh and resumes his homeward journey.

This is the most overtly descriptive of all Sibelius's tone poems. The links with the Legends is unmistakable, especially in the elements of magic involved. Väinämöinen, the ageing magician, is one of the leading heroes of the *Kalevala*; his failure, or that of his magic powers, greatly distresses him, not only because it deprives him of the greatly desired maiden but also because it exposes his own limitations. But he does not give way to sorrow and despair but continues his homeward journey knowing that 'the memory of sweet sounds brings hope and eases pain'.

Pohjola's Daughter appeared in 1906; in the same year Sibelius wrote the incidental music for Hjalmar Procopé's play *Belshazzar's Feast* which demonstrated his gift for evoking

Programme of a 'Sibelius evening', Helsinki, 25 November 1906, containing new material ('nya manuscript').

unusual and exotic atmospheres and locations, in this case the oriental. The music is not self-consciously 'exotic' and the orientalisms are restrained; but there is no mistaking its provenance. Sibelius clearly enjoyed writing it and embroiling himself in his friend's drama about goings-on in the Babylonian Court.

Two years later came more incidental music, this time for the Swedish Theatre's production of August Strindberg's *Swanwhite*. More typical Sibelius theatre music, the quality variable but much of it stamped with its composer's hallmark.

Yet all the time it was the Third Symphony that continued to dominate his mind and attention. To some extent its reception disappointed him; he was in the habit of referring to it later in his life as 'the beloved and least fortunate of my children', and certainly it has always been, along with the Sixth, the least often performed and appreciated of his symphonies. It was not so much the initial reception that disappointed him as the habit of neglect from which it subsequently suffered.

There is a sense in which the Third Symphony may be justly regarded as a 'transitional work', the marked transition being that between the comparative opulence of the first two and the austerity of the Fourth. The Third may be regarded as the most 'classical' of the series, but it remains pure and absolute Sibelius. Its apparent 'simplicity' is deceptive; both structurally and emotionally it is a good deal more complex than it may seem at first hearing. (It is also extremely difficult to conduct satisfactorily; the opening bars contain traps into which conductors tend to fall with great facility, and the middle movement is elusive in a way which frequently baffles both performers and auditors, especially in our present literal-minded age.)

The true significance of the Third Symphony in the overall context of Sibelius's life and art is only revealed in full by the succeeding works.

Early in 1908 Sibelius became increasingly worried by pains in his throat. Diagnosis revealed a tumour. At first it was thought to be non-malignant, but subsequent investigation suggested that it was not. Surgery was necessary; it appeared to be successful but for many years Sibelius lived in constant fear of a recurrence of cancer. Indeed it was necessary for him to go through a succession of operations, a dozen in all, before time and medical expertise freed him from nagging anxieties. For a whole decade he gave up two of his greatest private pleasures, cigars and alcohol. The way he was able to eschew the latter as he did casts doubts on the idea that he was seriously addicted and that one reason for the silence of his last thirty years of life was alcoholism. Certainly he was always a heavy drinker; but when he decided that he should give it up he did so, totally and without apparent difficulty—which is hardly the way of a confirmed alcoholic.

Exactly how much the dark fears and anxieties of his health were responsible for the austere character of the Fourth Symphony is difficult to judge. But the musical postulates of the Third were also leading in that direction, so that much of the character of the Fourth can be seen as a logical development of his art from the inside. It is always dangerous to read too much from a composer's life into his compositions; on the other hand there can be no possible doubt that his apprehension over his health did impinge upon the nature of the symphony.

Whatever the reason, the Fourth Symphony came out as the epitome of the Sibelian ethic and aesthetic. It enshrines within its four comparatively brief movements the essence of the composer Jean Sibelius. If the layout in four distinct movements appears, both in the retrospect of the Third Symphony and looking forward to the coming Fifth, as a kind of retrogression on the part of a composer whose evolving reputation is in the region of concision and the fusion of the separate elements of traditional symphonic structure it is not really so at all. That 'logical connection between all the motifs' which to Sibelius was of the essence of the true symphony is as prominent a feature of the Fourth as of any other composition by him. Part of the disturbing effect produced by this work is the reliance on the tritone in its evolution. The tritone is the interval of an augmented 4th, for instance the three whole tones F-B, the *si contra fa* which challenges the perfect fifth. In medieval times it gave rise to the expression '*Mi contra fa diabolus in musica est*' (Mi against fa is the devil in music'). It is difficult to sing, was taken to suggest evil in music, and was thoroughly discouraged in the old days. For Sibelius at this time, full of apprehensions over his throat condition, *diabolus* was clearly more than *in musica*, in nature itself as like as not. However, the tritone was no stranger to Sibelius's music; it appears in several earlier works, including the first two symphonies. It is its absolute predominance in the Fourth which is striking and unnerving. It tends to infuse the entire symphony with a kind of mutating malignancy.

Another reason why the Fourth Symphony caused puzzlement and a certain dismay when it first appeared in 1911, and still does in some quarters, is the way Sibelius compresses and foreshortens symphonic structure at least as far as it will willingly go, if not farther. This is the orchestral symphony stripped to the bone; not an ounce of superfluous flesh is left: some could even call it emaciated. Here Sibelius, to change the metaphor, composes entirely with musical nouns and verbs: not an adjective or adverb

Serge Koussevitsky, conductor of the Boston Symphony Orchestra and an ardent promoter of Sibelius's music.

in sight, hardly even a conjunction. It seems to foreshadow in music some of the subsequent developments in literature—elements of Ernest Hemingway's sparest prose for example. It is an extraordinarily concentrated work, and it requires the utmost concentration from both performers and listeners. The conductor, the late Serge Koussevitsky, once turned to his Boston audience who had received the Fourth Symphony coolly and told them that if they did not like it he would go on playing it until they did (he carried out that intention); and Herbert von Karajan says that it is one of the three works he finds most emotionally exhausting to conduct.

In a letter to Rosa Newmarch, Sibelius declared that his Fourth Symphony was 'a protest against the compositions of today . . .

nothing of the circus about it'. This was a large and not quite accurate claim: there were other composers around who were reacting against post-Wagnerian excesses and 'laughable would-be profundity' and writing music also spare and concentrated, though the description of his own symphony was accurate enough. Sibelius, in short, was moving in his own way and on his own terms into the modern world — in a number of ways anticipating its most notable features.

The Fourth Symphony was first produced in England at Birmingham in 1912, Sibelius himself conducting. It puzzled most people and was not heard in London until March 1920. On that occasion the *Musical Times* reported:

Arnold Bax: English composer who greatly admired Sibelius and was admired in return by him.

An important orchestral event was the playing at the Queen's Hall Symphony Concert of Sibelius's Fourth Symphony . . . It was not received with any favour then [at its Birmingham première], and it hardly proved more acceptable on this occasion, in spite of the care obviously lavished upon it by Sir Henry Wood.

Ernest Newman was present at that first Birmingham performance and he tells a revealing little story about one of the rehearsals.

At that time the Fourth Symphony was 'rather a tough nut for the English to crack':

A man whom I did not know seated himself beside me and looked curiously at my score, apparently in the hope that the evidence of his eyes might help to supply the understanding that has escaped him on the evidence of his ears alone. When the rehearsal was over he said to me: "Queer stuff, isn't it?' I tried to point out to him that his difficulty, which I was sure would only be a temporary one, was that this music came from a different national- and culture-heredity from ours: 'it comes from Finland,' I explained. 'Ah!' he said, with the air of one on whom the light has dawned: 'that's it: ah coom from Halifax myself.'

Since Sibelius himself was in Birmingham to conduct the première of the Fourth Symphony it is clear that notwithstanding his state of health and his operations, he was able to undertake another trip to England. In fact he did so in 1909, when he made further acquaintance with British musicians including Arnold Bax and Eugene Goossens, and was able to hear a fair amount of contemporary music being played at that time in London. He also paid proper attention to his own composing, and to the presentation of his own works to a public that was becoming increasingly interested in him and his music.

During 1909 he saw the first performance of one of his most imaginative tone poems, *Nightride and Sunrise*, completed work on his only published string quartet, *Voces intimae* (Intimate voices) and *In Memoriam*, a somewhat sombre 'public' piece which he intimated was written in memory of a young Finnish patriot, Eugen Schuman, who had assassinated a Tsarist official in 1904. *Nightride and Sunrise* was given its première in St Petersburg in January 1909. It is not one of Sibelius's deliberately 'Finnish' works in that it is not based upon the *Kalevala* or any similar source. Indeed, it has no programme and is not intended to have one. Sibelius himself said that he had no intention of writing 'romantic programme music' in the style of Raff and others. He somewhat disingeniously described it as

. . . . . concerned with the inner experiences of an average man riding solitary through the forest gloom; sometimes glad to be alone with nature; occasionally awe-struck by the stillness or strange sounds that break it; not filled with foreboding; but thankful and rejoicing in the dawn and the breaking of day.

The Fourth Symphony has to be seen as the crucial work of this period; indeed, in more senses than one, of the whole of Sibelius's work. Its 'bleakness' and 'austerity' and the personal background did not cause it to be nicknamed the 'Cancer' Symphony, but it did earn it the name in Finland of *Barkbröd* in recollection of the times of hardship in Finnish history when the peasants were obliged to mix the bark of trees with their grain in order to survive. This impression of bleakness did catch the attention of many to such an extent that it became accepted as the characteristic of this symphony and indeed Sibelius as a whole. The *Musical Times* report of the 1920 London performance ended with this observation:

We were informed in an analytical programme that the *Scherzo* is merry and buoyant, which causes one to wonder what sort of music Sibelius would write if he were depicting melancholy discontent.

In fact, as we have come to realise long ago, the Fourth Symphony is by no means all gloom and desolation. There is a story that one day Sibelius was out walking with a friend when they came upon a sudden glow of sunlight on a valley. Sibelius stopped and, pointing to it, said: 'I have put that into my Fourth Symphony.' The exact passage he was referring to may be a matter of minor dispute; but the story does indicate that the sun had not entirely gone out of his life and his music, despite his dark fears and apprehensions over his health. Or perhaps it is just that, as Ernest Newman concluded in 1937, remembering his puzzled companion of 1912:

Since that epoch, thanks entirely to Sibelius, the distance separating Halifax from Helsingfors has been appreciably diminished.

The poet Johan Ludwig Runeberg: Sibelius set many of his poems as songs and one of them may have inspired the tone poem *The Bard*.

There is a clutch of smaller works surrounding the Fourth Symphony which throw additional light on his methods of composition. These include one of his 'minor' tone poems, *The Dryads* which he presented in Oslo, as well as what must be seen as the masterpiece among his smaller scale tone poems, *The Bard*. This is an extraordinarily concentrated and masterful little piece, clearly an offshoot of the symphony. Sibelius left no clue to what precisely he had in mind as he wrote it, but what is clear to any receptive listener is that, like the symphony, it is every bit as remarkable for what it leaves out as for what it puts in. In this, too, Sibelius was in spiritual and stylistic accord with the times (twentieth-century economy superseding nineteenth-century discursiveness). It may be, as Erik Tawastsjerna has suggested, that *The Bard* was inspired by a poem by Johan Ludwig Runeberg of the same name. But that is really neither here nor there: it is the musical substance of *The Bard* that counts, the quite extraordinary originality of it and its relevance to other works of Sibelius at this period.

Quite different but no less original and giving the lie to the idea of Sibelius's unyielding severity and remoteness from the world of human feeling and human aspiration, is another 'offshoot' (musically speaking) from these years, the suite for strings, tympani and triangle, *Rakastava* (variously translatable as 'The Lover' or 'Love Song Suite'). This too is full of Sibelius's characteristic melodic and harmonic manner; it is also a masterful example of his writing for strings, no doubt another legacy of his youthful ambition to be a concert violinist. The impression created here is quite different from that of *The Bard*, not to pinpoint that of the Fourth Symphony specifically; but it is no less remarkable and individual. It came out of a somewhat strange background: it began life—or rather its basic material did—as a piece for unaccompanied male voice choir which he wrote way back in 1893 and was based on an anthology of folk poetry by Elias Lönnrot and offered as the young composer's entry in a song competition—unsuccessfully, largely because it was too 'advanced' and too difficult for the choirs involved. Later Sibelius made other arrangements of parts of it, one for male voices with strings, another for *a cappella* mixed chorus. After that it had to wait until 1911 before Sibelius took it seriously in hand and produced this lovely suite for strings. Anyone who still thinks of Sibelius as a 'cold' composer, musically inoculated against any infection by human warmth and feeling, and especially against sympathetic understanding of anything so tender and fragile as young love, has only to listen with unprejudiced ears to *Rakastava* to correct once and for all any such impression, or misconception. Indeed, it is hardly too much to say that *Rakastava* alters the general perspectives of Sibelius's life and work much as *Die Meistersinger* alters those of Richard Wagner, though on a much smaller scale. (There are three named movements—'The Lover'; 'The Path of the Beloved'; 'Goodnight, farewell'.)

Despite his worries over his throat ailment, and no doubt because these worries gradually receded as medical prognoses appeared to restore his wellbeing, Sibelius continued to travel during these years, both throughout Scandinavia and farther afield. As we have seen he made more than one trip to England; he also spent time in Berlin and Vienna. He was in fact offered a post as professor of composition at the Imperial Academy of Music in Vienna. However, he declined, largely on patriotic grounds coupled with a particular liking for living in his house at Järvenpää. This was not the only offer he received from outside Finland, and turned down.

Sibelius in 1912.

During his 1912 visit to England he had undertaken to compose a new choral work to be conducted by himself in Gloucester Cathedral the following year. It seems that he also had ideas about making a more prolonged holiday visit to England. Unfortunately, he did not complete the promised choral work and did not return to England. Much more fortunately he did complete another work for the Cathedral, the beautiful and totally original *scena* for soprano voice and orchestra, *Luonnotar*, Op.70. This is another example of Sibelius not conforming to the convenient pigeon hole of popular misconception. It is also another instance of Sibelius drawing on the *Kalevala*, from the first Runo this time, and, like *The Bard*, a further example of those small but highly individual pieces clustered round the Fourth Symphony. It deals with the Finnish legend of the Creation and of the birth of the hero Väinämöinen who we have already encountered being bested by the beautiful lady in *Pohjola's Daughter*. Luonnotar is the 'virgin of the air' and

. . . slender and beautiful, is wandering solitary over the desolate wastes. She descends upon the waves. For seven hundred years she swam in every direction; then a mighty wind arose and the waters rose. In her distress she called upon Ukko, the God of All.

There came a wild duck seeking a place to make her nest; but the wind and the waves buffeted her until she cried out against them. Then

73

Luonnotar stretched out her knee and received the eggs into her lap. A fire coursed through her and she took the eggs into the water. Lo! the eggs were broken into myriad pieces and the uppermost parts became the heavens, the white shone as the moon and the coloured parts became stars in the sky.

Perhaps one might see *Luonnotar* as a kind of continuation of the Fourth Symphony, since the final bars of the symphony have all that feeling of desolation and the desolate wastes Luonnotar encountered before she descended upon the waves to swim for those seven hundred years.

Whatever of that, *Luonnotar* remains one of Sibelius's most subtle and original compositions. It shows among other things the full scope of his writing for the voice and the demands he made upon it—which is no doubt why it has never been among the most favoured and why for many years it was scarcely performed at all. If only Sibelius had followed up this little masterpiece into the realm of opera or music drama, what a magnificent outcome there might have been.*

In fact Sibelius wrote vocal music throughout his life. He wrote many songs, some orchestral but most with the customary piano accompaniment. He may not have been one of the world's great song writers, fit to stand beside the German masters of the *Lied*, but he was an accomplished song composer in his own right and left a fair number of memorable examples, the texts mostly Swedish, with some Finnish and some German. Not surprisingly, in view of his overall musical sympathies and aptitudes, his songs are more in the bardic—*ie* declamatory—style than in the folk-derived manner of the German *Lied*. And *Rakastava* notwithstanding, his favourite subject is not young love and ardour but the evocation of nature in many moods and colours.

Sibelius also wrote a quantity of choral music, mostly accompanied by the orchestra but sometimes unaccompanied, of which the fine and powerful *Origin of Fire* for baritone solo, chorus and orchestra is a notable example, though by no means the only one.

But whatever else he may have written in whatever form and

---

*As a matter of fact, although Sibelius abandoned *The Building of the Boat* (see page 27), he did at the same time (1896) write a rather charming little one-Act opera, *The Maiden in the Tower* (*Jungfrun i tornet*) to a text by Rafael Herzberg. It made no great impression, is hardly prime-cut Sibelius though it has its passing attractions, and as a largely occasional piece it sank quietly into oblivion. It remained unpublished and was more or less dismissed from his memory by Sibelius. It has, however, been recorded quite recently.

for whatever medium, Sibelius's reputation will always rest upon his music for orchestra. He may not have been a more or less exclusively orchestral composer as, say, Wagner, Verdi and Puccini were exclusively operatic composers; on the other hand, everything he wrote apart from the orchestra was in a very real sense incidental (even *Luonnotar,* an undoubted masterpiece and despite the subtlety and originality of the vocal line is as much dependent on the orchestra for its unique effect as on the voice).

During 1913 Sibelius received an invitation to visit America. At first he declined the offer, but eventually reversed his decision

A remarkable family likeness: Sibelius's brother Christian as a young man.

and prepared to set forth. At the same time he received a commission for a new work from the musical authorities in Norfolk, Connecticut. Although the work intended was to have been a new choral piece for the Norfolk Festival, what emerged was another orchestral tone poem, *The Oceanides,* the only work of his that was not related in any way to Finnish or Nordic lore. It bears practical witness to another of Sibelius's life-long loves, that for Greek and Latin classical culture. *The Oceanides* is based on Homer and refers to the nymphs who lived in the waters of classical antiquity. It is an unusual piece for Sibelius, exploiting orchestral sonorities not found elsewhere in that form. He wrote the work in 1913/14: he began work on it in Berlin, revised it back home in Finland, took it with him to the US when he travelled there in May 1914 and conducted it in Norfolk on 4 June. It is in its way sea music, water music anyway, and it is possible that when in England he had heard an early performance of Arnold Bax's *The Garden of Fand* which was written around that time and has a number of similarities to *The Oceanides* which may have caught the sensitive ear of Jean Sibelius.

In America Sibelius stayed with Mr and Mrs Carl Stoeckel. It was Carl Stoeckel, a prominent patron of the arts, who had engineered the invitation to Sibelius and had commissioned the new work. Sibelius greatly enjoyed his American stay. He found, partly to his surprise and much to his delight, that he was famous and recognised in the States and was honoured wherever he went. He was given an honorary degree by Yale University and found American hospitality as warm and generous as he had previously found the English variety nearly a decade earlier. He was so well pleased with all he saw and experienced that he entertained serious ideas about making a prolonged concert tour of the US, as much as anything in order to pay off his ever mounting debts, as well as those of his brother Christian who seems to have been as dedicated and efficient a debtor as he himself was. In every way his time in America was unusually happy and rewarding. Sadly, it was destined to remain a cherished memory for him; he was fated not to return. This was the summer of 1914 and only a month ahead the clouds that had been gathering over Europe for years finally burst.

Chapter 4

Crisis of Civilisation

Look at the great nations of Europe and what they have endured. No savage could have stood so much. I do believe in civilisation

—*Jean Sibelius*

Programme of chamber concert held Helsinki 6 December 1915, including first performance of Sonata Op.80.

When the clouds burst, most of the nations of Europe and many beyond were engulfed. Even those that were not immediately involved were destined soon to be sucked in to a greater or lesser extent. To begin with, Finland was not directly involved though the repercussions were soon felt, inevitably in view of the physical proximity and historical involvement of one of the major combatants, Tsarist Russia.

For Sibelius himself, apparently safe in his private haven at Järvenpää, the consequences were soon to become dire. His music had made good progress in Germany and through his publisher Breitkopf & Härtel a large proportion of his income came from that source. But Germany was now at war, Finland was not a signatory to the Berne convention on copyright, so although his compositions continued to be played in many parts of the world the performing rights were not protected and consequently his royalties all but dried up. The entries under his name in Breitkopf's catalogue ran to nearly twenty-five pages and some vigorous promotion before the outbreak of war resulted in an ever-increasing recognition of and interest in his music. Things had begun to go really well for him, but the coming of war put an end to all that: his association with Breitkopf & Härtel virtually ended—at the very least it was drastically curtailed—and openings for new compositions seemed few and far between. He was obliged to do routine work in order to survive. He had always written a fair amount of 'light music', popular piano and other instrumental pieces, song etc. Now in order to keep the pot boiling his output in this department considerably increased. But he did not neglect 'serious' composition. Despite the troubled times and his financial difficulties he appears to have been in a reasonably cheerful and optimistic mood. He began work on a fifth symphony and made new publishing arrangements with the Danish firm of Hansen (now linked in London with J & W Chester).

After the dark penetrations of the Fourth Symphony the Fifth seems at first sight and hearing to mark some kind of return to the outgoing 'heroic' mood, though not to the musical structure, of the first two. In form and structure it is nearer to the Third. In the Third Symphony the biggest movement was the Finale and carried a stage further the fusion of two types of movement which Sibelius superficially inherited from Beethoven but made especially his own. In the Fifth Symphony it was the first movement that carried on this process, with its compound structure of first movement and scherzo so adroitly dovetailed

Sibelius with daughter Ruth and wife Aino at home in 1915.

Jean Sibelius performs his latest compositions. Programme for concert with the Helsinki Symphony Orchestra, 8 December 1915 (Sibelius's fiftieth birthday), which included the premiere of the first version of the Fifth Symphony. *Aallottaret* (Okeaniidit) is the Finnish name for the tone poem *The Oceanides*.

and integrated that only close analysis can determine not so much where one ends and the other begins as the overall identities of both. The middle movement here—also as in the Third Symphony though of a totally different character—is a form of intermezzo and the bold Finale in which, in Donald Tovey's graphic phrase 'Thor swings his hammer', makes the kind of conclusion that those who see Sibelius through the perspectives of the first two symphonies and the more extrovert tone poems had come to expect.

Some have seen (or rather felt) nautical motions and implications in the Fifth Symphony. There is no evidence that Sibelius intended any such thing: on the other hand, there is a kind of nautical swagger in many parts, a hint to the more fertile imagination of the nautical gait in some of the rhythms and body movements. Be that as it may, and it is not very important anyway, the Fifth Symphony is a work of much richness and creative vitality. Coming as it did on the heels of the Fourth, it tended to reverse a few misconceptions about the composer and his 'gloom' that were trying to circulate in the wake of the Fourth.

The Third Symphony ended with a large, complex and bipartite Finale; the Fifth began with a similar type of movement in a different context. It is thus possible to see the Third, Fourth and Fifth symphonies as a species of aesthetically and emotionally linked triptych with the Fourth as the meat in the sandwich between two flanking evolutions, all three leading in their own particular directions and reaching their individual musical conclusions. There is no evidence that Sibelius ever thought of them as such, but hindsight (which is by no means always to be despised) suggests that such a relationship is implicit.

Sibelius was approaching his fiftieth birthday as the war dragged on. He completed the Fifth Symphony—or rather the first version of it—in time for that landmark which was treated with much celebrating and turned virtually into a national occasion in Finland. If as a depressingly familiar rule prophets go unhonoured in their own country, that was never true of Jean Sibelius. The occasion of his fiftieth birthday brought forth a virtual inundation of gifts, congratulations and all the jolly junketings invariably associated with such an event where a much-loved public figure is involved. Even the Tsar went so far as to honour him (if a little tardily) by bestowing upon him the title of Professor.

The day of the Tsar, however, was all but run. In 1917 The Russian Revolution deposed the Tsar and altered the course of history. Meantime Sibelius remained preoccupied with the Fifth Symphony. He revised it in 1916—and again in 1919—and when it arrived at its final version, the one we know and hear today, it

At work in 1915.

Opposite page:
Outside Ainola with family.

was on his own admission virtually a new composition.

The revolution in Russia leading to the accession to power of the Bolsheviks also brought strife and military activity to Finnish soil. The anti-Left formed themselves into the 'White Guards' in order to forestall revolutionary risings; the Left-wing elements formed the 'Red Guards' to promote precisely that idea. When the Bolshevik government was installed in power Finland was proclaimed an Independent nation state. But in early 1918 the Red Guards attempted to seize power and turn Finland into a Russian satellite. There was fierce resistance with the result that Finland became torn by civil war. Predictably Jean Sibelius was on the side of the White. As a composer of overtly patriotic music he was looked upon with severe disfavour by the Reds, and for some time he was in direct physical danger. When the Reds captured Järvenpää his house was searched for concealed arms and other practical demonstrations of 'anti-revolutionary' sympathies, as though he was expected to be found concealing bombs, bullets and hand grenades under his bed or in his and his wife's small clothes.

The fighting, as in all civil wars, was bitter, savage and merciless. The quotation which heads this chapter is double-

80

edged and yet again begs a number of questions. It leaves out the small matter of how much of that which the great nations have endured is self-inflicted. And if the savage—or Rousseau's 'noble savage'—has not endured, or had to endure, so much, it is largely because he has lacked the means, though not the will or the inclination, to inflict such sufferings upon himself. Belief in civilisation was hard enough to maintain between 1914 and 1918 (and in the decades following), and if 'the great nations of Europe' actually did endure 'so much' it was hardly a tribute to civilisation or any of its processes but to human stupidity and gullibility.

The war raged on, Finland was ravaged by internal strife. Sibelius's situation steadily declined. Eventually he was persuaded to leave Järvenpää and seek refuge with his brother who was a doctor in the Lapinlahti Hospital in Helsinki, a psychiatric unit where some relief might be expected. In fact, in this Sibelius was largely disappointed. The Reds entered the capital and took over the hospital. Everything was scarce especially food, and the opposing guns were landing shells in the

Daughters Heidi and Margareta.

streets outside. Finally the Germans lent assistance against the Reds; the Whites triumphed and Finland was officially proclaimed an autonomous republic. The pressure, or the worst of it, relaxed, Sibelius was able to go home and get on with his work.

These were the outside circumstances which surrounded the Fifth Symphony. In a sense, therefore, it could be seen as a kind of creative riposte to the idiocies of the world in general. Beyond Finland the Great War blundered on: Thor's hammer continued to swing and thunder in innumerable unmusical ways.

82

The war over at last with much of Europe in ruins, even more emotionally and spiritually than purely physically, Sibelius was left to pick up the threads as best he could. During those years of war and revolution he had been cut off from the larger world of European and American musical activity. He was also separated from the great European and American orchestras through which he could expect to hear first-class performances of his compositions. It touched him and caused him distress and he did not cease to regret it. Nor did the restoration of European musical resources come automatically with the cessation of hostilities. There were wounds to be healed there as well as in the social and political bodies of those nations which had been in the front line of the fight. Germany writhed under defeat, France had been bled almost white, Russia was still caught in the trials and tribulations of the aftermath of revolution. Everywhere there was bitterness, vengefulness, perpetrated animosity. It did not bode well for the future despite many fine-sounding words, much rhetoric and many high hopes—and as it turned out the wounds were not healed but only scarred over with lingering festerings underneath.

But in 1918-19 it was the present rather than the future which occupied men's attention and required an immediate mending process. For Jean Sibelius it was no different—the necessity of rebuilding a life and a career.

As well as the final version of the Fifth Symphony, which was accomplished in the autumn of 1919 and given its first performance under the composer's baton in Helsinki on 24 November, Sibelius travelled around Scandinavia performing his works and thinking about new ones. He fulfilled a few official functions and sometimes provided music of an occasional nature for them, including a cantata, *Jordens sång,* for the inauguration of the Swedish Academy at Turku. These immediate post-war years appear at first sight to have been busy, but in fact they were more in the nature of a prelude to the real busyness of the early 1920s; a short period of recuperation and revitalisation after the disasters of the war years.

In 1920 Sibelius was offered a lucrative post in the USA, as professor of composition at the new Eastman School of Music. At first he decided to accept but never actually took up the post although the terms were highly favourable. Instead he made his last visit to England, in January 1921. It was on this occasion that he renewed his friendship with Busoni with whom he re-indulged his taste for high life and good living, to such an extent that Sir Henry Wood recorded how the pair of them became more or less unmanageable, failed to keep appointments and generally made life difficult for all persons who legitimately expected more punctilious behaviour from two distinguished musicians in their mid-fifties. Both were unrepentant, predictably, and for Sibelius in particular these were memorable days. He was never to meet his old friend and companion again, as Busoni was to die only three years later, aged only fifty-eight.

During 1921-2 Sibelius composed a further amount of his lighter pieces, including some charming orchestral sweetmeats like the *Suite mignonne*, the *Suite champêtre* and the *Suite caractéristique*, plus more miniature genre pieces for piano. The piano was never his natural instrument, but he wrote competently for it, as well as quite prolifically, though never on anything like the scale of his orchestral symphonies and symphonic poems. They brought him money and gave him pleasure. They are not much heard today, but they are an essential part of Sibelius's output, especially that part of it upon which he had to rely for his subsistence when times were harder than usual.

Alongside these various activities Sibelius's creative mind was constantly occupied with thoughts of at least two new symphonies. Stepping back a year or two we find him writing in a letter in 1918:

My new works—partly sketched and planned. The fifth symphony in a new form—practically composed anew, I work at daily . . . The sixth symphony is wild and impassioned in character. Sombre with pastoral contrasts. Probably in four movements with the end rising to a sombre roaring of the orchestra, in which the main theme is drowned. The seventh symphony. Joy of life and vitality, with *appassionato* passages. In three movements—the last an 'Hellenic rondo'. All this with due reservation . . .

In the event the 'due reservations' tended to predominate. Neither the Sixth nor the Seventh Symphony turned out as predicted. Whatever Sibelius may have had in mind at the time of writing that letter, it mostly came out very differently after it had properly gestated and been 'laundered' in his creative mind.

The letter does suggest however that Sibelius did see the three symphonies—the final version of the Fifth, the Sixth and the Seventh as—if not an actual trilogy—at least emanating from similar areas of the contemporary creative faculty. It in no way negates the suggestion that the real trilogy or triptych lies with and in symphonies Three, Four and Five. Whatever he may have said or written at any particular time or in any specific context, the musical deductions lead to the latter conclusion.

The Sixth Symphony, which appeared in 1923, and was given its première by Sibelius himself on 19 February in Helsinki, is neither 'sombre in character' nor does it end with any kind of 'roaring in the orchestra'. The previous month Sibelius had undertaken a concert tour through Norway and Sweden and soon after the presentation of the Sixth Symphony set out for Italy, where he conducted his Second Symphony in Rome and at the same time worked on his next, and as it turned out his last, symphony—the Seventh.

All that remained from the letter pertaining to the Sixth Symphony was the 'pastoral elements'. It has sometimes been called Sibelius's 'Pastoral' Symphony. There is truth in it, but not very profound truth. Certainly the Sixth, like all Sibelius's music, has a strong sense of the imminence of Nature: if 'naturalistic' would be too strong a word, it is not so wide of the mark as to constitute a vague irrelevance. In Sibelius the human personality confronts animate Nature, frequently at its most hostile; it also confronts the physical and metaphysical hostility of the emergent twentieth century. In the Sixth Symphony it is a kind of peace, at least a kind of armistice, that is achieved. Perhaps when he wrote the 1918 letter, he was more aware of the unavoidable aspects of the confrontation. In any case, the character of the Sixth is several removes from that of the 'tub-thumping' Sibelius of popular legend, not to say popular illusion.

The Sixth Symphony, like the Fourth, is in the traditional four symphonic movements. But it is in no sense a 'reversion' to traditional procedure or to anything else. As in the Fourth Symphony the interlocking of motifs is subtle and far-ranging. Indeed, the Sixth is the subtlest of all Sibelius's symphonies, one of the subtlest of all his works in fact—and Jean Sibelius is not generally recognised by the world at large as a particularly subtle symphonic composer. In the Sixth Symphony the voice is hardly ever raised and there is a marked absence of 'roaring'. But there is no lack of inner strength. The overall impression is one of power in repose.

Like Beethoven before him, Sibelius became increasingly interested in the music of Palestrina as he matured, and it often showed its influence in his music. It shows in the Sixth Symphony in particular, with its frequent recourse to modal textures, especially to the Dorian mode as in the opening pages. In fact this was nothing particularly new in Sibelius. From the beginning his music tended to be coloured and infected by aspects of modality. But in the Sixth Symphony it comes to a head and establishes its rightful place in the totality of his art. Much the same thing happened in the late string quartets of Beethoven. Sibelius was not a naturally polyphonic composer; but his entire technique led him towards the increasingly 'interweaving', as it might be called, perhaps in some ways via Bruckner.

The association of the names of Jean Sibelius and Anton

Sibelius in 1923 at the time of the Sixth Symphony.

Bruckner may not come immediately to mind. But as long ago as 1911 Sibelius wrote in a letter:

> Yesterday I heard Bruckner's B flat major Symphony, and it moved me to tears. For a long time afterwards I was completely transported. What a strangely profound spirit, formed by a religious sense. And this profound religiousness we have abolished in our country as something no longer in harmony with our time.

The Sixth Symphony of Sibelius far from being 'wild and impassioned' has something of that spiritual quality Sibelius discerned in the Fifth Symphony of Bruckner, though it is more related to Nature than to any formalised creed or religion.

As Wilfrid Mellers has observed: 'Sibelius, like Delius, had a religious sensibility without a faith.' That is why the Bruckner Fifth so moved him, and why so much of his music gives the unmistakable impression of a sensitive spirit confronting a predominantly hostile environment.

Perhaps part at least of the resolution is to be found in the succeeding Seventh Symphony. Both Cecil Gray and Constant Lambert discerned in this last of Sibelius's symphonies certain 'Olympian' qualities hardly to be found elsewhere in contemporary music, and rare in any age; a 'lofty grandeur and dignity, a truly Olympian serenity and repose' (Gray). It appears to represent in that sense not a retreat from the conflict but a kind of transcendence of it for, as Lambert rightly observed in his famous and influential book, *Music Ho!* first published in 1933:

> There is a repose which marks a final victory and a repose which marks an early defeat. Not everyone who renounces the world is a Buddha.

Musically the Seventh Symphony is not less remarkable. It is in one continuous movement and it seems to sum up in itself not only Sibelius's experience of life in several different directions, but just as much his experience of composing orchestral symphonies. Seen in the retrospect of his total output the Seventh Symphony combines the interlocking of motifs in the four movements of the Fourth and Sixth Symphonies and the formal integrations of the Third and Fifth. To some extent of course this, like all technical matter, is primarily for the specialist and the student; but it is also important for the general listener since it 'places' the work in the context both of the specific composer and of that listener's overall experience of music.

At first Sibelius called the Seventh Symphony a 'Fantasia Sinfonica' under which title he presented it in Stockholm in

March 1924, but he soon changed his mind and gave it its proper title. As the 'Seventh Symphony' it soon caught on, especially in America where both Leopold Stokowski and Serge Koussevitsky took it up.

Perhaps part of the key to the Seventh Symphony's musical and spiritual character is to be found in the reference in the 1918 letter to 'an "Hellenic rondo" '. This suggests that Sibelius's mind was orientated towards the Greek classical world he so admired and which he had loved all his life. Taking his life and work and the strenuous times through which he had lately lived, also in view of his general attitude to life and his belief that 'classicism is the way of the future', it could be that Sibelius was mindful of Nietzsche's tenet that the essence of Greek civilisation was 'the conquest of pessimism through art'. If that is so, then it would appear to lend further weight to the contentions of Gray and Lambert as well as to his own remarks in the 1918 letter about 'joy of life and vitality'. Either way, the Seventh Symphony stands as the final testament of one of the last great masters of the orchestral symphony, the one singled out by Arnold Schoenberg as being, along with Dimitri Shostakovich, the only significant symphonist of the age (Schoenberg might also have included the Dane Carl Nielsen; but Nielsen was so overshadowed for many years by Sibelius that his reputation outside Denmark had hardly made any progress).

Additional light is thrown on the musical and spiritual implications of the Seventh Symphony by the other work on which he was engaged concurrently, *Tapiola*, the last and greatest of his orchestral tone poems. In some ways *Tapiola* is an even more remarkable composition than the Seventh Symphony. It originated in a commission from New York and was premièred there by Walter Damrosch on 26 December 1926. Sibelius himself was not present for, as we have seen, he never did return to the US after his successful visit in 1914.

Tapiola is one of those compositions which invariably makes a powerful impression but in superlative performance can be overwhelming. Wagner said of the Third Act of *Tristan und Isolde* that if it was properly rendered it would 'make people mad: only bad performance can save me'. If the Cavatina of Beethoven's string quartet in B flat, Op. 130, is really played *adagio molto espressivo*, it can be almost unbearably poignant and we understand why Beethoven said the memory of the emotion it aroused always cost him a bitter tear. So *Tapiola*, when played to its utmost is so chilling and devastating that it shakes one to the core. It has been well said that it is scarcely to be endured when one is alone.

In Finnish mythology Tapiola is the informing spirit of the

Northern forests. The often quoted superscription on the score defines the provenance:

Wide-spread they stand, the Northland's dusky forests,
Ancient, mysterious, brooding savage dreams,
Within them dwells the Forest's mighty God,
And wood-sprites in the gloom weave magic spells.

With *Tapiola* Sibelius virtually ended his composing career, Between it and the Seventh Symphony, in 1925, he wrote the last of his theatre music, the incidental music for a production by the Royal Theatre, Copenhagen, of Shakespeare's *The Tempest*. This, although uneven, is the most substantial as well as the latest of his incidental music to dramas. It contains some of his subtlest and most imaginative music for the theatre. The best of it is in the line of his latest symphonic music. As in the Sixth and Seventh symphonies there are modal implications—but these, as I have said, are long established features of Sibelius's style, by no means confined to his late works—and full of his equally long established resourcefulness of scoring.

Since the advent of the cinema broadcasting and recording, 'live' orchestras have virtually disappeared from the theatre. A few events arise from time to time which bring back memories of the old ways and more popular forms of entertainment such as the 'musical' and the variety theatre (itself if not in direct decline at least in the process of continual change) still use 'live' music, and the currents of active nostalgia even occasionally bring back a 'live' pianist or two to accompany the old silent films, suitably refurbished; but overall music and the theatre have parted company. Music for the films has long since taken the place of music for the 'live' theatre; consequently there is little, if any, call for the kind of music Sibelius and many composers before him composed and frequently delighted in composing. It might be an exaggeration to claim that Sibelius's music for *The Tempest* was the last of its kind of any substance by an otherwise mainly 'serious' composer, but it would not be all that far off the mark.

In any case, much theatre music, like much film music, is inevitably and properly what it says it is—incidental. Too powerful and demanding music of this kind only detracts from the impact of the drama being enacted on stage or screen, even if it does not kill it altogether. We are all too familiar with the kind of 'incidental' music which merely detracts and distracts, especially in films and television. Since the invention of the 'talkies', the cinema, and by inference the television, has forgotten what the theatre knew at least from the days of the ancient Greeks—the value of silence.

It is therefore inevitable that a great deal of incidental music for the theatre must be what is known as 'pattern music', that is, music which is not intended to stand on its own feet away from its original purpose and is there to reinforce rather than create a particular situation and does so precisely by not drawing attention to itself. Not all of it inevitably needs to be of this description: in the right place and at the right time music of autonomous quality and genuinely original inspiration is not only acceptable but positively required—otherwise composers of the stature and quality of Sibelius would not be interested in writing it.

That Sibelius was strongly attracted to his commission for *The Tempest* music is demonstrated by the extent of the material he provided for it and by the quality of several of the items. The full score runs to some two hundred pages of manuscript in all, in thirty-four sections. As it thus stands it remains unpublished; but Sibelius extracted from it a Prelude and two orchestral suites. The original calls for a chorus as well as orchestra (since the Royal Theatre in Copenhagen was and remains an opera house it had greatly increased resources for musical presentation over an ordinary theatre and the requirement of a chorus would have caused no headaches and provoked no protest). The score specifies a 'small orchestra', but in fact except in respect of the expanded nineteenth-century orchestra of, say, Mahler and Richard Strauss, Sibelius demands forces that would have nonplussed any of the 'classical' composers from Mozart to Mendelssohn and might have given even Berlioz cause for a passing thought or two, since the requirement in the original includes three flutes and piccolos, three clarinets, two oboes, bass clarinet, two bassoons, four horns, three trumpets, three trombones, tuba, tympani, a substantial percussion section, harp, harmonium, plus of course the chorus. The two Suites are somewhat reduced from all this; but the fact remains that for *The Tempest* music Sibelius wrote his most extended theatre score and the most lavish.

Not everything, predictably, is on the highest level. All the same, the best is amongst the best written by Sibelius anywhere. The Prelude presents a representation of a storm as powerful and evocative as any in music, excelling even the storm music of Beethoven and Verdi, let alone the myriad examples produced by less exalted composers throughout history. The Prelude has been described as 'the most thoroughly onomatopoeic stretch of music ever written' (it recurs in curtailed form at the end of the first Suite); and the most 'inspired' items in both Suites, like 'the Oak Tree', the 'Intrada and Berceuse' in the first Suite, and the 'Chorus of Winds' in the second, are not easily forgotten, while numbers such as the 'Scene' in No. 1 and the 'Dance of the Nymphs' in No. 2 have much of the charm and delicacy of, say, the early *King Christian II* music. Most of the score contradicts Ralph Wood's exaggerated and contemptuous criticism of *The Tempest* music as 'a cascade of almost exhibitionistic virtuosity at last unclouded by any tincture of creative impulse'. Whatever else may be said about it, all these numbers, even the most conventional, sound unmistakably like Sibelius, if not at his best.

In the same way as *Tapiola* is the last of Sibelius's symphonic tone poems, and the Seventh is the last of his symphonies, the music for *The Tempest* deserves special attention as the last score he wrote for a medium he had cultivated throughout his life, namely incidental theatre music. There are those who argue that *The Tempest* is not his best score for the theatre though it is his most comprehensive and that the Seventh is not unreservedly his finest symphony (some would award that palm to the Fourth); but in each case the respective works contain his latest and most mature distillation of what he had been working on and towards over some forty years and are thus a kind of summing up of a lifetime's experience of life and art in relation to the times through which he lived, not as a remote and distanced hermit but in every sense as an active participant.

Chapter 5

Silence from Järvenpää

Exactly why Sibelius composed, or at least published, nothing of consequence after the final outburst of creative activity which produced the Seventh Symphony, *The Tempest* music, and *Tapiola* is a mystery that has never been solved. Many explanations, most of them purely speculative, have been advanced, and much ink has covered reams of paper in vain attempts to explain the apparently inexplicable. But nothing of

Ainola: Sibelius's house at Järvenpää.

substance has emerged. He had still a third of his life to live after the curtain fell on his creative activity in 1926 or thereabouts. He remained in reasonably good health for another thirty years and he maintained an active interest in the world around him, both musical and extra-musical. But no new works appeared, despite expectations aroused by rumours and more speculations. An Eighth Symphony was confidently expected. The 'first performance' was indeed apparently promised to a number of conductors, including Basil Cameron and Serge Koussevitzky. But nothing materialised. Sibelius's own laconic comment when questioned from time to time about it was the Swedish proverb: 'One does not sell the bearskin until one has shot the bear.' After his death his family announced that there were no new and unpublished works to come—and indeed, none ever did appear. So one is left with the conclusion that either he was not satisfied with the mythical 'Eighth Symphony' as far as he had progressed with it—and he did on more than one occasion intimate that the work was 'finished'—and exacted promises from his family that it be interned with him and never see light of day, or it had never progressed beyond the conceptual stage and remained a bright light only in its creator's eye. The internal evidence suggests that

Ainola: the interior.

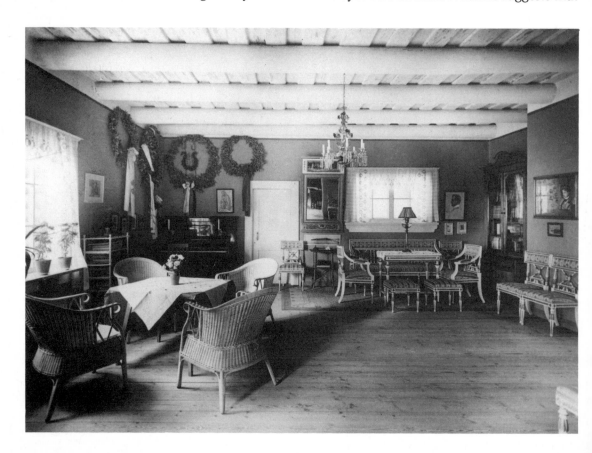

Sibelius in his garden during
his 'retirement'.

however he may have conceived the Eighth Symphony, it never did strike the germinating spark which set it alight and brought it to final fruition. Whichever way it was, the 'Eighth Symphony' never achieved birth let alone sparked animation. It remains a fable and a mystery, one among many where the latter life of Jean Silbelius is concerned.

Of the many 'explanations' that have been advanced for the failure not only of the Eighth Symphony but of anything else to appear during those barren thirty years, is that of chronic alcoholism. We have already noted that from his youthful days Sibelius was a heavy drinker: we have also noted that for a decade in the 1910s and beyond he abjured both alcohol and tobacco. Late in his life many people remarked on the extent to which he had the 'shakes' and had difficulty in writing or even holding things (including glasses) steady in his hands. The familiar deduction is that this was due to his 'drink problem', but from what has been written by associates and eye-witnesses it seems just as likely that it was due to some ailment in the area of Parkinson's Disease. Whatever it was, alcoholism seems to be only one possibility among several. Many incidents in his life testify to his strength of mind and character and even though drinking was a perpetual habit, if not a 'problem', even this he overcame in later life.

Another often advanced explanation for the long silence from Järvenpää (after the production of his last major compositions he gave up travelling and stayed at home) is that he increasingly felt that he had been left behind by the musical world and that people no longer wanted his kind of music.* This is exactly what seems to have happened in the case of Elgar in England. But there are significant differences between Sibelius and Elgar. For one thing, Elgar's creative spark was virtually extinguished by the death of his wife in 1920; for another, and a perhaps more important factor, Elgar's life and work had celebrated a world which reached and passed its zenith during his lifetime as England's star declined after the First World War, while Finland's came into the ascendant. In other words, it might be said that Sibelius was an active participator in the birth of a nation, while Elgar was a saddened spectator of the death of an Empire, the beginnings of that death anyway. How much either of these factors impinged directly on the musical relevance of their respective composers is

---

*Sibelius justified the austerity of his old age by saying that while other composers were engaged in manufacturing cocktails he offered the public pure cold water.

Neville Cardus, in *The Manchester Guardian*, 1938

a question that can never be answered, for it lies deep in the psyche of each and only impinges incidentally on the conscious response of either. That the musical world turned decisively in other directions after the First World War is plain historical fact and cannot be denied, even though it has to be remembered that all the *avant-garde* evolutions of music had not only begun but become established before 1914. All the same, it is undeniable that music such as Sibelius and Elgar wrote was 'out of fashion', Schoenberg and Stravinsky and their acolytes having established themselves as the young pretenders. But this applied largely to entrenched musical circles. To the larger public the music of the older generation, music such as Elgar and Sibelius and their like offered, was still more than acceptable. For this larger public the more 'modern' works were hardly received with enthusiasm, though Stravinsky's earlier ballet scores, including *The Rite of Spring* (at least to the more adventurous) had begun to percolate into the broader concert world. All the same, there were plenty still willing and eager to support the more 'traditional' compositions. But both Elgar and Sibelius were largely unaware of this; they did not know that their music was in demand and widely enjoyed—Elgar because he was old and tired and disillusioned, Sibelius because, tucked safely away in Järvenpää, he was simply unaware of the respect and affection in which he and his music were held by the general musical public, especially in America.

Whatever he may have felt and thought about the world outside and the musical condition of civilisation, he was certainly not downhearted. Or if he was he did not let it show to the many

Sibelius and Aino in 1927.

visitors he received with warmth and pleasure. There are innumerable stories about his outstanding hospitality and his capacity for enjoying good food and drink and good conversation. The English pianist Harriet Cohen wrote in her autobiography, *A Bundle of Time*, about a visit she and Arnold Bax paid Sibelius with Balfour Gardiner in the spring of 1932:

> Arnold and I had the gayest meeting with Sibelius at an outside restaurant sitting in the sun where I took their photographs, together and separately. We laughed and ate and drank, and the two composers, who liked each other on sight, got on famously. I remember noting how their talk veered round continually to history—a subject in which they were both interested. When the shadows lengthened we went to another favourite haunt of his, the Hotel Kemp, and we talked about literature, art and even world politics for hours . . .

Sibelius was a tremendous talker, as everyone who knew him testifies. He could, as has been often recorded, drink most of his companions under the table, but it was his stimulating talk which remains in many visitors' memories. But there was one subject he never discussed and never would discuss. On the subject of his own music he was invariably taciturn. He likened talking about his music to handling a butterfly: it 'crumbles at a touch. So it is with my compositions; the very mention of them is fatal.' It might be difficult to think of any major composition by Sibelius in terms of a butterfly, but that is how he felt about it and the point is taken. It also means that there is scant material to draw on in respect of his own comments on his work—yet there is a certain amount, a few hints and clues dropped here and there and picked up in passing by a sensitive ear or two.

He once reminded Bengt de Törne that the difference between the piano and the orchestra is that the latter has no sustaining pedal and that therefore it is necessary to write in sustained parts to create an artificial pedal. This throws a lot of light on Sibelius's orchestral methods. It also reveals the gulf between his method and Mahler's. Mahler loathed any suggestion of thickness in the texture. He himself often composed in what was virtually two-part counterpoint, producing the kind of 'hole in the middle' effect against which Sibelius specifically cautioned—which is perhaps one reason why Mahler dismissed Sibelius's music (or what he had heard of it at the time) as 'full of hackneyed clichés' during his visit to Helsinki in 1907.

This whole question is further illuminated in a conversation Sibelius had with Rosa Newmarch during her first visit to him in 1910. She and Sibelius had gone to see the Imatra rapids, the outlet of the waters of Lake Saïma:

Sibelius had at that time a passion for trying to catch the pedal notes of natural forces. The pedal note of Imatra no man has gauged, but Sibelius often seemed satisfied with the results of his rapt listening, when he caught the basic sounds of the forests, or of the wind whistling over lakes and moorlands. *

The enormous popularity of Sibelius during those years of the 1930s, even if he himself was not aware of it, had some curious consequences. To begin with, outside Scandinavia where it was always secure, it was largely confined to England and America. But more than that, it has often been claimed that the 'exaggerated' attention paid to Sibelius prevented any recognition of another great composer, Carl Nielsen, outside his

Sibelius with pianist Nikolai Orlow in 1931.

native Denmark. This is only in part true. A more profound reason for the neglect of Nielsen and the uprating of Sibelius was that, despite the unmistakable incidence of a 'Scandinavian' temperament, Nielsen was nearer in musical ethic and aesthetic to Mahler than to Sibelius—and Mahler, too, had to bide his time for full international recognition. Apart from the purely musical fact that Nielsen, like Mahler, used a form of 'progressive tonality' in part inherited from Wagner, and that his handling of

---

*Give me the loneliness either of the Finnish forest or of a big city.

Jean Sibelius, quoted in Layton, *Sibelius* (1965)

97

the orchestra was more *concertante* than *organum*, Nielsen himself once said, in the context of his own Fourth Symphony which has the subtitle the 'Inextinguishable': 'Music is life, and like life, is inextinguishable.'

This is a far more Mahlerian than a Sibelian remark and relates back to Mahler's counter to Sibelius: 'The symphony must be like the world, it must contain everything.'

The relationship between Mahler and Sibelius in the post-Second World War years makes another interesting and illuminating study. Even before the Hitler war, Sibelius had come to seem to many people old-fashioned and reactionary. After it, especially as he had contributed nothing new for more than a decade and in the light of the upsurge of post-Webern serialism, he held no interest at all for the 'progressive' and 'forward-looking' musicians of the day. (Both terms are somewhat question-begging and unsatisfactory since, again, both are invariably taken to mean only what the user wants them to mean.) Mahler, on the other hand, became the darling of contemporary fashion largely because diligent research discovered that he had not only been admired by Schoenberg and Berg but had actually been the precursor of full-blooded serialism.

Sibelius shaking hands with Wilhelm Furtwängler in 1950.

That none of this directly affected the average concert-goer and

98

record-buyer was for a time beside the point. But such persons, who may be identified as Ernest Newman's 'plain musical man', invariably in the end follow the dictates of fashion, even at a respectable distance.

Thus the reputation and popularity of Jean Sibelius declined at precisely the same time as those of Gustav Mahler rose. Exactly how much all this impinged on the consciousness of Sibelius, locked away in his northern fastness is difficult to determine. But in view of the two composers' altercation in 1907 it may well have had its indirect effect.

To the end of his life Sibelius maintained an interest in the musical world around him. In particular, he kept a wise and wary eye on the contemporary interpretations of his music.* He gave overt support in particular to those Finnish conductors like Tauno Hannikainen and later Okko Kamu who showed a genuine insight into and sympathy for his musical idiom. But in fact it was not specially, even primarily, the Finnish conductors who predominated. After Walter Legge had taken him the proof pressings of Herbert von Karajan's recordings of the Fourth and Seventh Symphonies and *Tapiola*, he said:

Karajan is the only man who really understands my music: our old friend Beecham always makes it sound as if he had learned it and conducted it from the first fiddle part.

This is another illuminating remark, especially since Beecham had long been recognised as one of the world's foremost conductors of the music of 'Old Sib', as Sir Thomas invariably called Sibelius. In fact Sibelius was not the only one to remark on this aspect of Beecham's conducting. The late Sir Neville Cardus once made much the same accusation in person to Sir Thomas in respect of Wagner. Sir Thomas at first protested innocence, then relented and replied in effect: 'Oh well, and why not? It's the best part anyway!' This of course is the exact opposite of Wilhelm Furtwängler's practice. Furtwängler always preferred to conduct from the basses upwards, which is why all his performances had such firm foundations. Unfortunately Furtwängler conducted very little Sibelius, like most leading German conductors of the day. Indeed, the lack of appreciation and performance of his

---

*He was thought by his closest associates to be psychic — 'not dependent only on five senses,' as his secretary put it. His wife believed he was aware when one of his works was being broadcast anywhere in the world. 'He is sitting quietly reading a book or newspaper. Suddenly he becomes restless, goes to the radio, turns the knobs, and then one of his symphonies or tone-poems comes out of the air.'

works in Germany was still another source of sorrow and disillusion to Sibelius in the years of his silence. Before the First World War Germany had been one of the principal sources of his European success, and his association with the publishing firm of Breitkopf & Härtel had been happy and profitable. But after the war German musical life turned to the experimental and in many respects the 'revolutionary' and left the apparently 'traditional' Sibelius unplayed and unloved. It was a big disappointment, even though he probably understood the main reasons for it. None of the leading German conductors—Furtwängler, Klemperer, Kleiber, Bruno Walter—espoused his cause and he felt the cold-shouldering intensely, at least until von Karajan took him up and became one of his leading advocates. Before that time—which came in the early 1950s—his main champions were English or American: Beecham, Henry Wood, Malcolm Sargent; Koussevitsky, Stokowski, sometimes Toscanini—with the British Anthony Collins leading the way with the first complete post-war cycle of recordings. He never did make much headway in Latin Europe: in immediately post-war Europe it was still possible to hear him referred to in amateur music circles as *inconnu.*

If the history of Sibelius's life and times up to about his sixtieth year was the history of his travels and his compositions, after the mid-1920s it was largely the history of his reputation in its variegated aspects and that of performances of his works, plus his already legendary hospitality and the recollections of his many visitors.

However, Sibelius's peaceful retirement was rudely interrupted by the outbreak of the Second World War in 1939. At first, again, Finland was not directly involved in hostilities. But the signing of the Nazi-Soviet treaty some months before, which many saw as an act of treachery on Stalin's part and as promoting the outbreak of war, boded no good for anyone, Finland least of all. In the light of history, the perspectives have become not quite as clear as they seemed at the time. One immediate consequence was that Stalin immediately set about securing Russia's western frontiers. If the treaty was on the surface designed to do this, no one took it seriously, least of all Russia. A little mutual back scratching, though, did neither party any immediate harm. But things were not as they appeared. Perhaps Stalin had read *Mein Kampf* and understood that Hitler's ultimate objective was always war with Russia. However it was, the two powerful sides ranged if not immediately against each other, at least in preparation for various eventualities. And this of course involved Finland.

Stalin's first move was virtually to annex the Baltic States of

Latvia, Lithuania and Estonia by familiar strong-arm tactics; the next was to try the same on Finland. Threats and demands which could not be met—and which everyone knew could not be met—left the Finns in an impossible position. The Russians demanded the lease of a base on the island of Hangö on the north side of the Gulf of Finland; occupation of the western portion of the Rybachi Peninsula which gave access to the port of Petsamo, Finland's only Arctic port; and to take territory in Karelia, which would have been strategically disastrous for Finland and deeply offensive to Finnish national feeling. Inevitably the demands were rejected out of hand and no less inevitably provoked an

Field Marshal Carl Gustav Mannerheim: the Finnish national hero who commanded the Finnish army against the Soviet invasion of 1940. Before that he had been prominent in national affairs.

Sibelius at the time of his ninetieth birthday.

'incident' and Russia launched a military attack on Finland in November 1939.

The world watched, partly puzzled, partly in astonished anger. The full implications and ramifications of this apparently inexcusable act of aggression were not understood at the time: all the outside saw was a brutal assault by a large and powerful nation on a small and supposedly weak one—which is what many thought the larger war was mostly about. In the event, of course, things did not go as expected or predicted. The Finns, under the command and brilliant generalship of the national hero Field Marshal Mannerheim, not only resisted but inflicted a series of bloody noses on the Soviet armies. It could not last and it didn't: sheer weight of numbers and material in the end prevailed and Finland was forced to succumb. And inevitably the Finns suffered greatly.

Much of the world's attention was directed to seeking news of the welfare and whereabouts of Sibelius, Finland's other leading national hero. The First World War had caught him at the prime of fifty years; the Second found him moving, as he and the world at large expected, into serene and undisturbed old age. Many rumours circulated, some that Sibelius was in mortal peril (which were almost certainly true in one sense or another), one even that he had been killed in an air raid (which was mercifully not true). What is certain is that he and his family suffered much privation. He received many offers to take refuge abroad, but would not consider it. He did make a radio appeal for help from America and a postage stamp was issued with a picture of his head and bearing the message: 'I need your help.' It was all he could do; it was all anyone could do. There was much public popular demand in the West for practical (*ie* military) assistance to be sent to Finland. But however willing governments and peoples may have been to help, it was virtually impossible. Petsamo had fallen into Russian hands so there was no access by sea, and intervention by air was at that time beyond effective possibility. As it turned out it was probably as well: there was no Allied force available although several countries, including France, had serious thoughts about it, and there was not the proper equipment anywhere and no time to assemble it or to train the personnel necessary for such an operation. Any attempt to go to Finland's assistance out of natural sympathy or political expediency would almost certainly have resulted in total failure, which would have done a lot more harm than good all round. It was one of those fortunate and providential circumstances which saved more than face.

In the end, what happened was that Finland, at last overcome by immense numerical superiority, was forced to accept terms—which included surrender of territory in Karelia—and taught the Russian armies things they needed to learn and in fact did learn. From the Allied point of view the only material consequence was that the fate of Finland had a direct bearing on the subsequent Norwegian campaign.

Through all this Sibelius lived avoiding as far as he could the worst ravages of time and warfare. He survived, though in exactly what material shape was unclear. There were reports that he and his family were in serious need. These appear to have been false—or at least considerably exaggerated. He celebrated his eightieth birthday in 1945 while the restrictions and tribulations of war were still active. But his eighty-fifth was again an occasion for national as well as family rejoicing. His ninetieth birthday in 1955 was another of the same with a strong international addition, with tributes and presents reaching him from England (Winston Churchill suitably honoured the day in kind as from one dedicated cigar smoker to another) and America. In Finland the celebrations were nationwide. Public and private tributes poured in from all manner and classes of people from the President downwards.

Sibelius and Aino at home.

During these latter years of his life Sibelius lived quietly with his family—there was a bevy or covey of daughters, grandchildren and great grandchildren, though they were not all invariably there at the same time—but not always as privately as he would have wished. By nature a quiet and reserved man, he hoped to live out his days in peace and tranquility. But he had long since become a 'public celebrity' and public celebrities are never left in peace and never were. With the easing of travel and other restrictions after the war, Sibelius found both his home and his person objects of international curiosity and organised pilgrimage. Tourists tried to invade his privacy and often physically invaded his premises. He took measures to preserve his privacy, as far as he could without contradicting his natural warmth and liking for welcoming and entertaining visitors.

In spite of this, his last years remained reasonably peaceful. His health had always been a curious mixture of robustness and delicacy. At the time of his marriage to Aino Järnefelt in 1892 he seems to have been in somewhat uncertain health, to such an extent that she was warned that she was taking on a potential invalid. That may have been so; but he lived until past his ninetieth birthday and from all outward appearances enjoyed good health for most of the time. Certainly his old age was not

104

President Paasiviki: he broadcast a message on the occasion of Sibelius's ninetieth birthday.

troubled by more than the normal complement of passing ailments which in the course of nature beset the elderly. He was in reasonably good form until the day of his death.

A man who lives past ninety years is certain to lose many good friends and associates along the way. It was so with Sibelius and it did nothing to restore his self-confidence and creative wellbeing. Among the most serious losses of old friends and lifelong supporters were those of Axel Carpelan who had died in 1922, Robert Kajanus who departed in 1933, and Granville Bantock who went in 1946. These and other losses depressed and discouraged him, and as he grew older and passed into his eightieth and ninetieth decades the casualties inevitably mounted. The years took their inevitable and remorseless toll and, coupled with the traumas of war and revolution and their attendant miseries, darkened a number of aspects of his later life.

On the credit side was the growing appreciation of his music in America which slowly percolated through to him at Järvenpää; the formation of the Sibelius Society by HMV in 1932; and the obvious affection in which he was personally held by musicians and many non-musicians throughout the civilised world. Although he had given up foreign travel in the 1920s, he continued to conduct his own works locally. He was not an enthusiastic conductor as in their different ways Elgar and Richard Strauss were. He was certainly not a master interpreter of all music as Gustav Mahler had been; but he was a good conductor of his own music. He frequently premiered his compositions and, according to report, usually made an effective impression, even if he did need the preliminary assistance of a half-bottle of champagne before he could, in his own words, 'conduct like a god!' Unlike Elgar he did not leave a sizeable legacy of recordings of his interpretations of his music, so that we have

Programme of a concert by 'Society of Lively Musicians' given 18 March 1961 which included the item *Heita, koski, kuohuminen* from one of Sibelius's 'left sketches'.

only a few words dropped along the way to indicate his thoughts on, in the words of Igor Stravinsky: 'the composer's wishes in respect of the music.' There is one tiny item on record conducted by Sibelius, the *Andante festivo*, but although there were embryonic plans for more substantial contributions, these came to nothing and were never likely to do anything else. This was in 1934, when he was already confirmed in his retirement and would not be lured out of it.

On 20 September 1957 Sibelius's long life and long retirement came to an end. On that day Sir Malcolm Sargent was in Finland to conduct the Helsinki Symphony Orchestra in a performance of Sibelius's Fifth Symphony. In the early afternoon Sibelius collapsed. He had given no outward sign of failure, but his condition was swiftly diagnosed as a cerebral haemorrhage. He lingered through the afternoon, conscious and able to recognise members of his family; but during the evening, while Sargent was conducting the symphony, he died.

Predictably the funeral was impressive and a further occasion for national attention, the kind which attends the passage of all those who have left behind them good work well done. Naturally some of his own music was played, including *The Swan of Tuonela*, appropriately since it is not only one of his most enduringly popular pieces (and one specifically concerned with the subject of death) but also the one in which he first found his own true and authentic voice in music.

Some years previously his old conservatoire building had been converted and renamed after him and a Sibelius Museum was set up and remains to this day at Turku (Abo). Various scholarships and festivals continue to be held in his name and his honour, and places in various parts of the world bear witness by their names to his reputation and his memory.

He remained in many ways an enigmatic figure, both in his work and in his person. The composer Arnold Bax, after complaining about the undue attention paid to his slighter pieces which he, Bax, dismissed as 'with scarcely an exception, entirely undistinguished and characterless . . . There is precisely nothing to them. They are not even bad, and never vulgar . . .' wrote in the early war years:

And what of the old gentleman of Järvenpää nowadays? Since he no longer writes either masterpieces or rubbish can it not be that in happier circumstances his caprices would have become even more irresponsible as the years advanced, and his laughter still more Homeric? But, alas! there is nothing to laugh about in Finland to-day.

If he lived, especially in the last third of his life, an outwardly quiet and 'private' existence apart from two World Wars and their concomitant upheavals, the reality is not quite so simple. Inwardly his peace was hard won. To reach the serenity of the Sixth and Seventh Symphonies, deceptive though it may be at times, was a comparatively long and arduous road. And *Tapiola* at the very end of it may suggest that the snakes in the human mind and psyche are only scotched not killed: the repose that he did win was certainly not of the kind that marks an early defeat. Taking his life and work as a whole, Jean Sibelius has to be seen as one who looked into the abyss of the fermenting twentieth century, both musical and non-musical (and not only in Finland), and saw there some disturbing phenomena and alarming spectres.

But he did not flinch.

Sibelius's Works

The following list contains all the music the average listener is likely to encounter. Many of the slight pieces Sibelius composed and published throughout his life are seldom heard today and do not contribute significantly to the general enjoyment and understanding of his life and times.

Symphonies:
Symphony No. 1 in E minor, Op. 39 (1899)
Symphony No. 2 in D major, Op. 43 (1901-2)
Symphony No. 3 in C major, Op. 52 (1904-7)
Symphony No. 4 in A minor, Op. 63 (1911)
Symphony No. 5 in E flat major, Op. 82 (original 1915, revised 1916 and final version 1919)
Symphony No. 6 in D minor, Op. 104 (1923)
Symphony No. 7 in C major, Op. 105 (1924)
(Symphony No. 8: unfinished, unpublished and probably non-existent)

Symphonic tone Poems:
En Saga, Op. 9 (1892, revised 1901)
Four Legends, Op. 22 (original 1895)
Pohjola's Daughter, Op. 49 (1906)
Night-Ride and Sunrise, Op. 55 (1909)
The Bard, Op. 64 (1913-14)
The Oceanides, Op. 73 (1914)
Tapiola, Op. 112 (1925)

Miscellaneous orchestral music:
Karelia Overture, Op. 10 (1893)
Karelia Suite, Op. 11 (1893)
Spring Song, Op. 16 (1894)
Scènes historiques (first series), Op. 25 (1899)
Finlandia ('Finland awakes', with or without chorus), Op. 26 (1900)
The Dryads, Op. 45 (1910)
Dance Intermezzo, Op. 45 (1910)

Johann August Strindberg:
Sibelius wrote incidental music
to his *Swanwhite* in 1908.
There were fourteen numbers
in the original score from
which Sibelius extracted a
suite of seven items.

Pan and Echo (Dance intermezzo), Op. 53 (1906)
In Memoriam (Funeral March), Op. 59 (1909)
Scènes historiques (second series), Op. 66 (1912)
Three Pieces (*Valse lyrique; Autrefois, scène pastorale;*
   Valse chevaleresque), Op. 96 (1912-20)
Suite mignonne (2 flutes & strings), Op. 98a (1921)
Suite champêtre (strings), Op. 98b (1921)
Rakastava (strings & percussion), Op. 14 (1911)
Suite caractéristique (strings & harp), Op. 100 (1922)

Incidental music to plays:
King Christian II (play by Adolf Paul), Op. 27 (1898)

Kuolema (Arvid Järnefelt—as revised contains *Valse triste* and *Scene with Cranes*), Op. 44 (1903-6)
Pelléas et Mélisande (Maeterlinck), Op. 46 (1905)
Belshazzar's Feast (Hjalmar Procopé), Op. 51 (1906)
Swanwhite (Strindberg), Op. 54 (1908)
Scaramouche (Paul Knudsen), Op. 71 (1913)
Jedermann ('Everyman'—Hugo von Hofmannsthal), Op. 83 (1916)
The Tempest (Shakespeare), Op. 109 (1926)

Opera:
The Maid in the Tower (1896)

Violin and Orchestra:
Concerto in D minor, Op. 47 (1903-5)
Two Serenades (D minor & G minor), Op.69 (1912-13)
Two Pieces, Op. 77 (violin or cello) (1914)
Two Humoresques (D major & D minor), Op.87b (1917)
Four Humoresques, Op. 89 (1917)

Chamber Music:
Sibelius wrote a considerable amount of chamber music in his youth but little of it was published and his only mature contribution was:
String Quartet in D minor (*Voces intimae*), Op. 56 (1909)

There is also a good deal of music for violin and piano, published and successful in its day but not often heard nowadays.

Piano Music:
The piano was not really Sibelius's instrument, but he wrote an amount of music for it. The main items are:
Six Impromptus, Op. 5 (1893)
Sonata in F major, Op. 12 (1893)
Ten Pieces, Op. 24 (1894-1903)
Ten Bagatelles, Op.34 (1903)
Pensées Lyriques, Op. 40 (1912-14)
Kyllikki (three lyric pieces), Op. 41 (1904)
Ten Pieces, Op. 58 (1909)
Three Sonatinas, Op. 67 (1912)
Five Pieces, Op.75 (1914)
Thirteen Pieces, Op. 76 (1914)
Five Pieces, Op. 85 (1916)
Six Pieces, Op. 94 (1919)
Six Bagatelles, Op. 97 (1920)

Eight Short Pieces, Op. 99 (1923)
Five Romantic Compositions, Op. 101 (1923)
Five Characteristic Impressions, Op. 103, (1924)

Choral Music:
Kullervo ('Symphony'), Op. 7 (1892)
Rakastava (for *a cappella* male chorus), Op. 14 (1893)
Six Part Songs for *a cappella* male chorus, Op. 18 (1900)
Tulen synty ('The Origin of Fire' or 'Ukko the Firemaker'),
    Op. 32 (1902)
Five Part Songs for *a cappella* chorus, Op. 84 (1914-15)
March of the Finnish Jäger Battalion, for male chorus &
    orchestra, Op. 91 (1917)
Jordens sång ('The Song of the Earth'), Op. 93 (1919)
Maan virsi ('The Hymn of the Earth'), Op. 95 (1920)
Two Part Songs for male voice chorus *a cappella*, Op. 108
    (1925)
Väinön virsi ('Väino's Song') (mixed chorus & orchestra),
    Op. 110 (1926)

and a good deal else often of a strictly occasional nature.

Songs:
Sibelius wrote a large number of songs throughout his career. The
following is a list of the principal collections, with one or two
important single entries:
Five Christmas Songs, Op. 1 (1895)
Arioso (Runeberg—voice with piano or orchestra),
    Op. 3 (1893)
Seven Songs (Runeberg), Op. 13 (1891-2)
Seven Songs with piano, Op. 17 (1894-1903)
Koskenlaskjan morsiamet ('The Ferryman's Brides—baritone,
    or mezzo-soprano & orchestra), Op. 33 (1897)
Six Songs with piano, Op. 36 (1899)
Five Songs with piano, Op. 37 (1900)
Five Songs with piano, Op. 38 (1902)
Six Songs with piano, Op. 50 (1906)
Eight Songs with piano, Op. 57 (1909)
Eight Songs with piano, Op. 61 (1910)
Luonnotar (Tone-poem for soprano & orchestra),
    Op. 70 (1913)
Six Songs with piano, Op. 72 (1914)
Six Songs with piano, Op. 86 (1916)
Six Songs with piano, Op. 88 (1917)
Six Songs (Runeberg) with piano, Op. 90 (1917)

Sibelius on Record

George Schneevoigt, the Finnish conductor who succeeded Kajanus as director of the Finnish National Orchestra and recorded some of Sibelius's works, including the Fourth and Sixth Symphonies and *Luonnotar*.

It would certainly be a gross exaggeration to say that the international reputation of Jean Sibelius was created by the gramophone and its recordings; but it was greatly enhanced thereby. Unlike Elgar, Sibelius did not leave a legacy of his own recordings of his works. Although he conducted many of them in various parts of the world during his active lifetime and gave many, probably the majority, of first performances, he only left one example of his 'godlike' conducting on record, and that of nothing more substantial than the *Andante festivo*. There were plans for him to record a complete cycle of his symphonies and symphonic poems in 1934, but unhappily these never

materialised. As mentioned in the main text, the significant early moves were made first by the Finnish Government when it commissioned recordings of Sibelius's first two symphonies and the formation of the Sibelius Society in England by Walter Legge for HMV in 1932. These recordings exerted an enormous influence and have been transferred to LP. They are not currently available as they have been withdrawn from the World Records catalogue, but it is inconceivable that they will remain permanently out of circulation. They include Kajanus's versions of the first three and the Fifth symphonies and some of the tone poems, Beecham's classic version of the Fourth and Koussevitzky's Seventh. This leaves the Sixth out in the cold. This was recorded later by George Schneevoigt who succeeded Kajanus as conductor of the Finnish National Orchestra in 1933. Schneevoigt also recorded the Fourth Symphony but that did not meet with Sibelius's approval: he much preferred Beecham's, as he preferred Beecham's Sixth recorded much later (1946) but never transferred or re-released after its initial 78rpm issued on HMV, apparently for contractual reasons (it originated from RCA in America). In addition there is Heifetz's magnificent reading of the Violin Concerto with Beecham conducting. Apart from the Schneevoigts, all the recordings had the stamp of Sibelius's personal approval, so that although he did not leave any recordings of his own he left a very clear idea of how he wanted and expected his music to sound.

Also as mentioned in the main text, Sibelius considered Herbert von Karajan the best conductor of his music at the end of his life. Karajan has recorded all the symphonies except (at the time of writing) the Third, many of them more than once. They are among the finest and are becoming available on Compact Disc, considerably to their advantage. Particularly valuable is the re-coupling of the Fourth and Sixth Symphonies, two outstanding performances (DG). Hardly less valuable is the coupling of the Fifth and Seventh, ditto. The first complete post-war cycle of the symphonies and most of the tone poems was that by Anthony Collins for Decca, many items still available on Ace of Clubs or Eclipse. Other conductors who have made complete cycles are Leonard Bernstein (CBS), Lorin Maazel (Decca), Sir John Barbirolli (HMV), Paavo Berglund (HMV), Sir Colin Davis (Philips), all with many merits and most with some shortcomings. Among the younger British conductors who have addressed themselves to Sibelius in succession to Wood, Sargent, Barbirolli, Collins, Boult, Simon Rattle seems to stand pre-eminent: his versions of the First, Second and Fifth have been widely and justly praised, while his conducting of the Fourth in an illuminating analytical programme on television confirms his stature as a Sibelian. Sir Alexander Gibson has long since also so established himself with the Scottish National Orchestra (latterly recording for Chandos). Sibelius has been popular with the record companies and the leading conductors (especially British and American ones) since the 1930s and the choice is wide and rewarding to make, though in the cases of the latter their recorded legacy is less than we might have hoped, always excepting Leonard Bernstein whose cycle is always stimulating, sometimes outstanding (Fifth), occasionally somewhat less so (Fourth/*Luonnotar*). Currently Vladimir Ashkenazy is working his way through the repertoire for Decca in versions which are always admirably played by the Philharmonia Orchestra and splendidly recorded. The performances tend to please those who prefer a Russian/Slavonic view of Sibelius (especially in the earlier works) and are not put off by a good deal of self-indulgence. The Estonian conductor Neeme Jarvi is in the process of working his way through all Sibelius's orchestral music in a project planned to cover all of twenty-five issues, with the Gothenburg Symphony Orchestra (for BIS/Conifer). The Finnish conductor Paavo Berglund who made his cycle while director of the Bournemouth Symphony Orchestra and included in it the pioneering recording of *Kullervo* (HMV) has now repeated it with the Helsinki Philharmonic Orchestra with Finnish choir and soloists as part of a new complete cycle (also HMV). The tally of Sibelius recordings increases month by month. It never really eased off since the heyday of his reputation during the 1930s and 1940s; even during the years of the 'reaction' against him the flow of recordings did not abate (indeed, the Collins series for Decca appeared at a time when his standing was near its lowest among trendy critics). Some of the more outstanding recordings from American conductors remain in circulation, notably those by Stokowski, Koussevitzky and Eugene Ormandy as well as Leonard Bernstein, and although many of them are now a bit long in the tooth (or groove) modern refurbishings have frequently succeeded in giving almost legendary performances and recordings continuing leases of active life.

Of Sibelius's other music there are several first-class recitals of songs from singers who understand what is required of them by him and these, too, are increasing in numbers. An excellent example is the album of orchestral songs, which includes the incomparable *Luonnotar*, by Mari-Anne Häggander and Jorma Hynninen and the Gothenburg Symphony Orchestra (BIS/Conifer).

The permutations of Sibelius recordings are almost endless, the choice enormous, and many, as I say, are finding their way onto

Leopold Stokowski, another of Sibelius's most active champions in America who made a number of recordings of his music.

Compact Disc. The interested collector of Sibelius must, in the end, choose for him or herself, for as always it is bound to come to a subjective preference. There is one issue, however, that should not be overlooked, though it too easily can be, and that is an HMV album (not CD'd) entitled *The Lighter Sibelius* by the Royal Liverpool Philharmonic Orchestra under Sir Charles Groves, now on HMV 'Greensleeves' ESD 1062274 (tape TC-ESD 1062274). It contains many of the smaller orchestral pieces including *The Dryads*, *Pan and Echo* and the Suites *mignonne* and *champêtre*. Some of these items show how hard Sibelius tried to repeat the success of *Valse triste* and one or two of them—*Valse romantique* and *Canzonetta*—demonstrate how near he might

116

have come to it with a little bit of luck. Apart from this record most of these pieces are not likely to be heard more than once or twice in a lifetime of concert-going except by the most dedicated devotees.

The String Quartet in D minor (*Voces intimae*) appeared in the old Society lists by the Budapest Quartet; it is available in several modern versions. An interesting issue is that by the Sibelius Academy Quartet which contains two early string quartets—in E flat major and B flat (Op.4) not otherwise heard and only barely acknowledged by Sibelius himself. They add to our offbeat appreciation of Sibelius's art, but do not contradict the idea that *Voces intimae* is his only relevant piece of chamber music (Finlandia/Conifer records). Selections of Sibelius's piano music come from Erik Tawastsjerna (BIS/Conifer).

In the plethora of modern recordings of music of all and every kind, even Sibelius's little one-Act opera *The Maiden in the Tower* has found its way onto Compact Disc—and proves to be rather an unexpected delight, even if hardly major Sibelius.

Select Bibliography

Sibelius literature in Finland and Scandinavia generally is copious and far ranging. By no means all of it is available in English or other translations but it all tends to be important one way or another. For present purposes a select list of the most illuminating books, either originally written in English or available in translation, will suffice. For those who wish to probe deeper into the matter there is *Jean Sibelius: An International Bibliography on the Occasion of the Centennial Celebrations, 1965*, compiled by Fred Blum and published as No. 8 of the Detroit Studies in Music Bibliography by Information Service, Inc, Detroit, USA with a note on books on Sibelius published since 1965. I divide the selections into two parts: books on Sibelius himself, biographical and critical; general music books containing significant material on Sibelius in a larger context. In both cases books marked (*) are mentioned or quoted from in the main text.

I.

Abraham, Gerald (Ed.): *Sibelius: A Symposium*, London, 1947, 1952.

Arnold, Elliot: *Finlandia: The Story of Sibelius*, New York, 1950

Ekman, Karl: *Jean Sibelius: His Life and Personality*, (trans), London, 1936; New York, 1938

Gray, Cecil: *Sibelius*, London, 1931 (*)

Hannikainen, Veikko: *Sibelius and the Development of Finnish Music*, (trans) London, 1948

James, Burnett: *The Music of Jean Sibelius*, London, 1983

Johnson, Harold: *Jean Sibelius*, New York, 1959; London, 1960

Layton, Robert: *Sibelius*, London (Dent 'Master Musicians'), 1965

Le Brecht, Norman: *The Book of Musical Anecdotes*, London, 1985 (*)

Newmarch, Rosa: *Jean Sibelius: A Finnish Composer*, 1906

Newmarch, Rosa: *Sibelius: A Short History of a Long Friendship*, Boston, 1939; London, 1945 (*)

Tawaststjerna, Erik: *Jean Sibelius* (4 Vols), 1965-78 (Trans)

Törne, Bengt de: *Sibelius: A Close-Up*, London, Boston, 1937 (*)

Karl Ekman, Finnish writer on music who published a biography of Sibelius in 1935.

II.

Abraham, Gerald: *A Hundred Years of Music*, London, (1938) 1964

Bax, Arnold: *Farewell My Youth*, London, 1943 (*)

Cardus, Sir Neville: *Ten Composers*, London, 1945

Cohen, Harriet: *A Bundle of Time*, London, 1969 (*)

Copland, Aaron: *Our New Music: Leading Composers in Europe and America*, New York and London, 1941

Downes, Olin: *Olin Downes on Music*, New York, 1957

Gray, Cecil: *A Survey of Contemporary Music*, London, 1924

Grout, Donald Jay: *A History of Western Music*, London, 1960

Hill, Ralph (Ed.): *The Symphony*, London, 1965

James, Burnett: *An Adventure in Music*, London, 1967

Lambert, Constant: *Music Ho!*, London 1936 (*)

Mellers, Wilfrid: *Man and his Music* (Vol. 4), London, 1967 (*)

Simon Parmet: Finnish conductor who worked many years in America. His study of Sibelius's symphonies, published in 1955, is influential and penetrating.

Myers, Rollo H: *Twentieth Century Music*, London, 1960

Newman, Ernest: *From the World of Music* and *More From the World of Music*, London, 1956, 1958 (*)

Scholes, Percy (Ed.): *The Mirror of Music* (extracts from the *Musical Times*), London, 1944 (*)

Schonberg, Harold C: *Lives of the Great Composers*, New York & London, 1970

Schwarzkopf, Elisabeth: *On and Off the Record: A memoir of Walter Legge*, London, 1982 (*)

Simpson, Robert: *Sibelius and Nielsen*, London, 1965

Thomson, Virgil: *The Music Scene*, New York, 1945 (*)

Tovey, Donald F: *Essays in Musical Analysis*, London, 1936-9

Wood, Henry J: *My Life in Music*, London, 1938

The Sibelius Museum

The Sibelius Museum is the collective name for the different sections of the Department of Musicology at Abo Akademi (Biskopsgatan 17, 20500 Abo 50, Finland), the Swedish language university of Turku. The Department comprises both the teaching section, where it is possible to study musicology up to the highest academic level, and the exhibition section with its collections of musical instruments. The library and the archives together with the collections of records are used equally by both sections.

The present Sibelius Museum was founded in 1926, when Professor Otto Andersson became the first to hold the newly established chair of musicology and folk poetry at Abo Akademi. Professor Andersson set about collecting materials connected with music and musical history, principally notes, instruments,

letters and pictures for his department library. The first instruments were donated in 1928 and at the same time Professor Andersson's own private collection of instruments was incorporated in the Department's collections at Abo Akademi, under which name they were known until 1949.

As early as the beginning of the 1920s those Sibelius materials belonging to Abo Akademi were included in the general collections. These included the score of the cantata *Jordens Sång* ('Song of the Earth') which Sibelius had written for the inauguration of the Akademi in 1919, and the first editions of many of Sibelius's works that had been published up to then. Those Sibelius manuscripts owned by Adolf Paul, a close friend and fellow student of Sibelius, were also purchased for inclusion in the collections.

The Sibelius Museum's collection of musical instruments now comprises approximately 800 items, mainly European instruments for the performance of 'high' music but also folk music instruments from different parts of the world. Most of these have been given to the Museum in the form of donations. About 450 instruments are on permanent exhibition, the remainder being kept in the Museum's storage space. The present Museum building was inaugurated in February 1968. Designed by the architect Woldemar Baeckman it is constructed largely of concrete and glass and laid out on two floors, the lower one lying below ground level. The volume of the building is 10,000 cubic metres and there are teaching and exhibition rooms on both floors. The archives are similarly to be found located on both floors.

A large part of the Museum's archive materials has been catalogued, but so far these catalogues have not been published so that it is necessary to use the card indexes on the spot. A total of eleven catalogues are currently available, including those devoted to Finnish note materials, handwritten manuscripts, letters, a Sibelius card index with 17 sub-headings, an instrument catalogue, catalogues of 78rpm records, 33rpm records, pocket scores, recorded tapes, books and pianola rolls. If necessary, some of the materials can be microfilmed (at the user's expense), and manuscripts and notes can, within certain restrictions, be copied. Collections are, in principle, open to any interested persons and enquiries should be directed to the Museum's secretary who is responsible for the entire archives.

The main Archives are divided into sections, including Press Cuttings and Photographs (sub-divided into 'Person' archive , Topographical archive, Other cuttings and photographs); Concert Programmes (national and international); 'Note' archive (Manuscripts and handwritten material, and published scores); Recorded Music archive; Collections of Letters; Photographic Negatives; Journals and Magazines; Pocket Scores; Books.

The above sections refer to general national Finnish culture and worldwide culture(s) in general. In addition there is, specifically and valuably, a large Sibelius card index dealing with the large and increasing quantity of material concerning Sibelius himself,

his life, his works and his general place in national and international history. This covers the whole of Sibelius's life and work and is the premier reference source for everything pertaining to him, in whatever context.

From the spring of 1986 the Sibelius Museum has had a comprehensive database of Sibelius's works, including all published compositions, literature, etc. The Museum's collections are increasing all the time: it continues to collect both old and new musical instruments (as well as toy, school and folk items), record players, radios, pictures associated with music, concert programmes, notes, gramophone records, manuscripts, letters, etc. The Museum is grateful to receive both donations and depositions.

Index

Illustrations are indicated in bold type and underlined

WORKS

See pp 109 et seq. also the following
references in the main text: